A FAITH FOR THE 1980s

A FAITH FOR THE 1980s

A guide to membership of the Church

J ROY H PATERSON

Illustrations by LILIAN McAULAY

THE SAINT ANDREW PRESS
EDINBURGH

This book was first published by J Roy H Paterson as *A Faith for the 1970s* and subsequently re-issued by THE SAINT ANDREW PRESS in 1972. It had two further impressions: in 1974 (with amendments) and in 1976.

Copyright © J Roy H Paterson, 1979

ISBN 0 7152 0433 5

Printed in Great Britain by Bell and Bain Ltd., Glasgow

CONTENTS

ACKNOWLEDGEMENTS

The extract from the poem 'The Creation' is from *God's Trombones* by James Weldon Johnson, and is reproduced by permission of George Allen & Unwin Ltd.

The extract from the hymn 'The Church is wherever God's people are praising' by Carol Rose Ikeler is reproduced by permission of The Westminster Press, Philadelphia, U.S.A.

INTRODUCTION

A guide to membership of the Church must be comprehensive without being exhaustive. It must also be the product of its age and kept up to date. This completely revised edition of *A Faith for the 1970s* takes into account the new thinking of the Church and of those becoming members of it in the 1980s. It is hoped, however, that it will also be useful to those who have been members of the Church in the past and who are looking for a book that will refresh their minds on the vows which they once took.

Obviously too this guide has its limits. It provides a very adequate introduction to the Christian faith and life but it does not expand on these. Some subjects are treated in greater depth than others but as each page stands on its own, there is no need for the reader to spend time on subjects that do not personally affect him or her. It is hoped, however, that the method of presentation and the clarity of the text and the illustrations will make each page equally attractive to read.

Various suggestions have been incorporated from those who have used the earlier editions and the present book introduces a number of pages in question form – to arouse interest and to provide opportunity for discussion in, say, an enquirers' or a new communicants' group. The material has been written by a Church of Scotland minister and while references are made to the practices of this Church, it is not to the exclusion of other Churches or other traditions.

A FAITH
FOR THE 1980s

A guide
to membership of the
Church

The Christian faith needs a GUIDE to understand it.

This book will not provide all the answers – but it will certainly help.

It may even raise further questions in your mind – but this is to help you to find a faith that is your own.

It is written in the hope and with the prayer that God will use it to make himself known to you and so help you to discover the life that is offered by Jesus Christ.

NEWS is what you get when you read the NEWSPAPER.

GOOD NEWS – and that is what the word GOSPEL means – is what you get when you read the Bible.

HAVE YOU A BIBLE?

It is important that you should have a Bible that has good print and is in a language that you can easily understand. Here are some good English translations.

The *AUTHORISED VERSION (AV)*, sometimes known as the *KING JAMES VERSION (KJV)*, was published in 1611. The language is very fine but may not be familiar to modern readers.

The *REVISED STANDARD VERSION (RSV)* was published in 1952. It is in good literary English and retains the style and language quality of the Authorised Version.

The *NEW ENGLISH BIBLE (NEB)* was published in 1970 and is written in modern English and in a fairly formal style.

The *GOOD NEWS BIBLE (GNB)* is a 'common language' Bible and is sometimes known as *TODAY'S ENGLISH VERSION (TEV)*. First published as a complete Bible in 1976, it has the widest circulation of any modern English translation. Unless otherwise stated, the scripture references in this guide are taken from the Good News Bible.

THE VOWS OF CHURCH MEMBERSHIP

'Your word is a lamp to guide me
and a light for my path'

Psalm 119:105

MEMBERSHIP VOWS

These vows have been authorised by the General Assembly of the Church of Scotland

1. DO YOU BELIEVE IN ONE GOD,
FATHER, SON AND HOLY SPIRIT;
AND DO YOU CONFESS JESUS CHRIST
AS YOUR SAVIOUR AND LORD?

2. DO YOU PROMISE TO JOIN REGULARLY WITH YOUR FELLOW
CHRISTIANS IN WORSHIP ON THE LORD'S DAY?

3. DO YOU PROMISE TO BE FAITHFUL IN READING THE BIBLE,
AND IN PRAYER?

4. DO YOU PROMISE TO GIVE A FITTING PROPORTION OF
YOUR TIME, TALENTS AND MONEY FOR
THE CHURCH'S WORK IN THE WORLD?

5. DO YOU PROMISE, DEPENDING ON THE GRACE OF GOD, TO
CONFESS CHRIST BEFORE MEN, TO SERVE HIM
IN YOUR DAILY WORK, AND TO WALK IN HIS WAYS
ALL THE DAYS OF YOUR LIFE?

THE CHURCH'S FAITH AND OURS

The Church has a faith

The faith of the Church is spelt out in its creeds. (The word 'creed' comes from the Latin *credo* which means 'I believe'.) These creeds are based on what Christians over many years have come to believe about God and Jesus. One of the earliest is to be found in a letter written by Paul.

> 'If you confess that Jesus is Lord and believe
> that God raised him from death, you will be saved.'
> *Romans* 10:9

It was not until about AD 200 that an official creed covering all aspects of the Christian Faith came into general use. This was known as the APOSTLES' CREED. It was not, of course, compiled by the apostles but it contains what is considered to be a summary of their faith. Though this is one of the ancient creeds of the Church it is still widely used and will be referred to frequently in the course of this book.

The Christian has a faith

The creeds help individual Christians to know what they believe. Belief is necessary for Christians because they live in two worlds – the world of the senses and the world of the unseen. They can see the world of the senses with their eyes but 'no-one has ever seen God'. (*1 John* 4:12). 'To have faith is ... to be certain of the things we cannot see.' (*Hebrews* 11:1).

The Christian faith is not based on a myth or a fantasy. It is built firmly on a fact of history – that a man of the name of Jesus once lived on this earth in a place called Nazareth. Christians believe that he was also the Son of God. The text-book for this faith is the Bible and in this guide all quotations from it are marked by a reference to the particular book, chapter and verse from which they are taken.

A MATTER OF BELIEF

The first vow (first part)

DO YOU BELIEVE IN ONE GOD, FATHER, SON AND HOLY SPIRIT?

'I believe I'm going to fall'

Everything we do in life is shaped and determined by what we believe. Our beliefs affect our attitudes as well as our actions. In the above picture the expression on the man's face is related to what he believes is going to happen when the bird has pecked through the branch.

Belief in a person is called 'trust'. We base our lives on the fact that people are to be trusted. The Bible tells us that God is to be trusted completely. This means that we can rely on him absolutely.

'Our ancestors put their trust in you,
they trusted you, and you saved them.'

Psalm 22:4

There is a good illustration of trust in *Mark* 9:14–27. It is about a man whose son was an epileptic and who believed that Jesus could cure him of his disease. 'Help us if you possibly can', he said to Jesus. Jesus replied, 'Everything is possible for the person who has faith.' 'I do have faith', said the man, 'but not enough.' But it was enough. His faith was perhaps no bigger than a grain of mustard seed. (See *Matthew* 17:20.) It was all that was needed. The young man was cured.

Do you know of anyone who needs the kind of help that this man needed? Do you believe that Jesus can still offer that kind of help today? Many people have found that he can. And all it needs is a mustard seed of faith.

A question of definition

There is a story told about a boy who was drawing on a large sheet of paper. 'What's that you're drawing?' his mother asked him. 'I'm drawing God,' he replied. 'But no-one knows what God looks like', said his mother. 'No, but they will when I'm finished!' said the boy.

People have different ideas about God and what he is like. Some would say simply that he doesn't exist. Others would question how it is possible to know him. Christians would claim that they have a special knowledge of him. Let us look at these different points of view.

THE ATHEIST POINT OF VIEW

An atheist is one who believes that there is no God. Man is the highest form of being. He is self-sufficient. There is meaning and purpose in his existence apart from God. This is basically the humanist position.

THE AGNOSTIC POINT OF VIEW

An agnostic is one who does not know if there is a God. In a poll on whether God exists or not, he would answer 'Don't know!' This could be an honest starting-point for many people who want to believe in God.

THE CHRISTIAN POINT OF VIEW

Christianity starts with a belief in God. A Christian does not try to prove that God exists. He accepts the fact that he does exist and puts his faith in him. Many non-Christians also believe in God—or in gods. Plato, the Greek thinker, once said, 'All men, Greek and barbarian alike, think that gods exist and behave as though they did.'

A Christian believes that God has made himself known to us in Jesus Christ. Paul said to the people of Athens, 'As I looked at the place where you worship, I found an altar on which is written "To an unknown God".' (*Acts* 17:23) He then went on to describe God who had made himself known in Jesus.

ONE GOD, FATHER, SON AND HOLY SPIRIT

ONE GOD...

In countries with a Christian tradition people might find it difficult to think in terms of more than one God. In pre-Christian times belief in many gods was commonplace. In the Old Testament we read that God had to remind his people that he was the only God and that his name was Jehovah (which means 'Lord'). 'I am the Lord', he said, 'there is no other God.' (*Isaiah* 45:5)

The Bible describes this God as a very personal being. His name 'Lord' implies that he has a distinct personality and character. This does not mean that he has a physical form or that he is visible. 'God is a spirit', said Jesus (*John* 4:24). 'No-one has ever seen God' (*1 John* 4:12). As a person he is able to think, to plan, to will and to love. This is what makes it possible for human beings to have a personal relationship with God. In the United States a telephone call to a particular person is known as a 'person-to-person' call. God has a direct line to each one of us and so we can talk to him on a person-to-person basis.

FATHER, SON AND HOLY SPIRIT

We can only know this one God as he has made himself known to us. The Bible says that God has revealed himself in three ways—as the Father, as the Son and as the Holy Spirit.

These three ways are sometimes referred to as Three Persons or as the Trinity. In this case 'person' is used in the sense of 'a player's mask' (Latin, *persona)* which actors wore to portray a particular character. By using different masks the one player could take on different roles. In the drama of life God wears three different 'masks'. He shows himself as three different 'persons' — as Father, Son and Holy Spirit.

Let us now look at each of these persons in turn...

ONE GOD, FATHER, SON AND HOLY SPIRIT

The Apostles' Creed says:

I BELIEVE IN ONE GOD; THE FATHER ALMIGHTY, MAKER OF HEAVEN AND EARTH

GOD IS FATHER

We have seen that God has a distinct personality and character. Jesus described this precisely when he gave God the name 'Father'.

Before Jesus' day people knew that God was good and wise and holy – but he seemed very far away. He was one to be honoured, revered and obeyed, rather than one to be loved. Even in the Old Testament, however, we read that God had the characteristics of a father.

> 'As kind as a father is to his children,
> So kind is the Lord to those who honour him.'
> *Psalm* 103:13

Jesus took the name 'Father' and transferred it directly to God. God is holy, he said, but God is also Father. And thus he taught his disciples to pray:

> 'Our Father which art in heaven,
> Hallowed be thy name.' *Matthew* 6:9, *AV*

In the *Good News Bible* this reads 'May your holy name be hallowed'.

The word that Jesus used for 'Father' was *Abba (Mark* 14:36). A rough translation of it would be 'Dad'. Jesus meant by this that our relationship with God should be as close and intimate as that of a child with his or her human father. St Augustine described the relationship in this way: 'God loves each one of us as though there was only one of us to love.'

The Lord's Prayer begins with the words 'Our Father'. We are to think of God as the Father of all of us. We belong to one family who acknowledge God as Father. The Christian faith is not just for individuals. It is a family faith.

8

GOD IS ALMIGHTY

God is not only Father; he is almighty, ie all-powerful. This does not mean that God can do anything. God cannot, for example, do anything that would be contrary to his own nature. He cannot do anything that a father would not do.

IN WHAT SENSE IS GOD ALMIGHTY?

God is almighty in that he has power over the forces of nature. The 29th psalm is a good example of this. We know too that Jesus – the Son of God – had that same power. When once he stilled a storm at sea, his disciples said, 'Who is this man? Even the wind and the waves obey him.' (*Mark* 4:21)

WHY DOES GOD ALLOW SUFFERING?

If God is almighty, one would not expect him to allow anyone to suffer. God, however, is also a Father who gives us the same kind of freedom as a human father gives to his children. A human father may teach his child not to run on to a busy road but that child of his own free will may do that which he has been taught not to – and get hurt as a result. Similarly, God – our Father in heaven – teaches us in Jesus how we ought to live but if we choose to go our own way, ie to sin, we may well have to suffer the consequences. Suffering, it should be noted, is not always related to the sufferer's own sins but it has to do with the fact that there is sin and evil in the world.

God is almighty in that he can take the sin and suffering of the world and use it for his own good purposes. He is like a potter who finds an imperfection in the clay he is working on and starts afresh with the clay to turn it into a different piece of pottery (see *Jeremiah* 18:4–6). In the same way God takes us with our imperfections and makes us into different people, better people. Having free will, however, we have to co-operate with God in this remaking of our lives. As Paul says, 'In all things God works for good with those who love him.' (*Romans* 8:28)

GOD IS MAKER OF HEAVEN AND EARTH

The first verse of the Bible tells us that 'In the beginning God created the universe' (*Genesis* 1:1). In *1 Corinthians* 8:6 we read that 'God, the Father, is the Creator of all things.' God made everything out of nothing but the best thing he made – his masterpiece – was man. After that 'God looked at everything he had made, and he was very pleased.' (*Genesis* 1:31)

The Bible says that God made the world in six days (see *Genesis* 1). Some see this as a description of the scientific origins of the world. The biblical writers, however, were not scientists. They were looking for an answer, not to the question of how the world was created, but why it was created. Their conclusion was simply that God made everything according to his own master plan and then – because he had no-one to share his enjoyment of what he had created – he made man. James Weldon Johnston in a poem called 'The Creation' tells how God by himself is lonely and needs us for companionship and fellowship.

... God walked around,
And God looked around
On all that he had made.
He looked at his sun,
And he looked at his moon,
And he looked at his little stars.
He looked on his world
With all its living things,
And God said, 'I'm lonely still!'
Then God sat down –
On the side of a hill where he could think,
By a deep, wide river he sat down;
With his head in his hands,
God thought and thought
Till he thought, 'I'll make me a man!'

God holds the world and us in the hollow of his hand but he has given us also creative powers. Man by his sin has destroyed much of what God has created. Now God looks to man – to us – to create his world afresh, and to make it the perfect place that it was in the beginning.

The Apostles' Creed says –

I BELIEVE IN JESUS CHRIST HIS ONLY SON OUR LORD.

WHAT'S IN A NAME?

When a baby is born, he is given a name. Usually the name is one which the parents like for one reason or another. In biblical times a name had a special meaning, usually a religious one. Thus today we might choose the name 'Dorothy' because it means 'Gift of God' or 'Christopher' because it means 'Christ-bearer'.

The name JESUS

In *Matthew* 1:21 we read that the angel said to Joseph concerning Mary: 'She will have a son, and you will name him Jesus – because he will save his people from their sins.' The name 'Jesus' means 'Saviour'.

The name CHRIST

In Jesus' day people didn't have surnames. A man would be known by the name of his father or by the place where he lived. Thus Jesus would be known as 'Jesus, son of Joseph' (in Hebrew, Jesus-bar-Joseph) or as 'Jesus of Nazareth'.

'Christ' is not a surname but a title. It should be prefixed by the definite article. As we speak of 'William the Conqueror', so we should speak of 'Jesus the Christ'.

The word 'Christ' meant 'the Messiah' or 'the Anointed One'. He was to be the one whom God would anoint as prophet, priest and king. The Jews thought that the Messiah would be some great conquering hero who would rescue them from their enemies. This is why they could not accept Jesus as Messiah when he was born as a baby in Bethlehem. Christians, on the other hand, believe that this baby was 'the Christ' or 'the Messiah'.

God's relationship to Jesus was such that it could only be described in terms of a Father and his Son.

> 'God loved the world so much that he gave his only Son'
>
> *John* 3:16

A son has a likeness to his father

We sometimes use the expression 'Like father, like son' or 'He's very like his father'. Jesus told his disciples that he was like his Father. 'Whoever has seen me has seen the Father' (*John* 14:9). He did not mean by this that there was a physical likeness. For a Jew 'son of' meant 'having the same nature as'. Jesus 'reflects the brightness of God's glory and is the exact likeness of God's own being' (*Hebrews* 1:3).

STORY OF A REFLECTION

In Rome there is a building where there is a picture called 'The Dawn'. It is by Guido Reni and it is painted on the ceiling of a room. Immediately below is a table with a large mirror in which the picture is reflected. This enables visitors to look at the picture without having to crane their necks. In the same way God the Father 'up there' is reflected in Jesus the Son 'down here'.

A son has access to his father

In everyday life it may be possible for us to meet someone whom we don't know through the person's son or relative whom we do know. Paul tells us that 'it is through Christ that all of us ... are able to come ... into the presence of the Father' (*Ephesians* 2:18).

ONE GOD, FATHER, SON AND HOLY SPIRIT

A Christian believes that Jesus was both God and man. He was completely divine but he was also completely human. It is difficult for us to understand how this is possible. The facts, however, bear it out and Christians in their own experience have found it to be true.

A Christian believes that Jesus was human

Those who knew Jesus during his earthly life recognised him as being no different from themselves. In Nazareth he was 'the carpenter, the son of Mary, and the brother of James, Joseph, Judas and Simon' (*Mark* 6:3). His way of life was the same as that of everyone else. He ate and slept, walked and worked, behaved like any other human being. And he understood people because he had been through the same kind of experiences as they had. Because of all this he was given the title 'Son of Man'.

A Christian believes that Jesus was divine

Those who knew Jesus intimately also knew that he was different from other human beings. He was always able to resist temptation. 'He was tempted in every way that we are, but did not sin' (*Hebrews* 4:15). Simon Peter said quite openly that he was 'the Messiah, the Son of the living God' (*Matthew* 16:16). 'Take Jesus as a man', said Martin Luther, 'and you will find that he is God.' Jesus' divinity was most evident:

(a) *in his teaching*

'The crowd was amazed at the way he taught. He wasn't like the teachers of the Law; instead, he taught with authority' (*Matthew* 7:29).

(b) *in his claims*

He said things that only the Son of God had a right to say, eg 'I am the way, the truth, and the life; no one goes to the Father except by me' (*John* 14:6).

(c) *in his power*

He had miraculous gifts. He could heal the sick. He even forgave men their sins and everyone knew that 'God is the only one who can forgive sins' (*Mark* 2:7).

The Apostles' Creed says:

I BELIEVE IN JESUS CHRIST HIS ONLY SON OUR LORD WHO WAS CONCEIVED BY THE HOLY GHOST, BORN OF THE VIRGIN MARY

Christmas Day marks the birthday of Jesus. Mary was his natural mother but it would appear that Joseph was not his natural father. 'His mother Mary was engaged to Joseph, but before they were married, she found out that she was going to have a baby by the Holy Spirit' (*Matthew* 1:18). God had made the circumstances of Jesus' birth unique.

SUFFERED UNDER PONTIUS PILATE, WAS CRUCIFIED, DEAD AND BURIED

This phrase was inserted to show that Jesus – though the Son of God – was 'well and truly dead'. The reference to the Roman governor Pilate gives the event its place in history.

HE DESCENDED INTO HELL

Jesus died on the day we call Good Friday. The Jews did not believe in life after death but they did believe that there was a resting-place for departed spirits. They called this place *Sheol*, in Greek, *Hades*, and translated here as 'hell'. It is not to be confused with the place where traditionally the wicked receive a fiery punishment after death.

THE THIRD DAY HE ROSE AGAIN FROM THE DEAD

Good Friday was the first day. Saturday, the Jewish sabbath, was the second day. The third day was what we call Sunday, the first day of the week. It was on this day that Jesus rose from the dead. We know it now as Easter Day. We commemorate it each week on Sunday, 'the Lord's Day' (*Revelation* 1:10).

The story of Jesus' resurrection is found at the end of each of the gospels. Various accounts are given of how he appeared to his disciples over a period of forty days. He was now no longer restricted by time or space. At the end of that period he gathered them together in Galilee for his final earthly appearance among them. Though they would no longer be able to see him, he told them 'I will be with you always, to the end of the age' (*Matthew* 28:20).

HE ASCENDED INTO HEAVEN

After these resurrection appearances, Jesus left the earth. 'He was taken up to heaven as they watched him, and a cloud-hid him from their sight' (*Acts* 1:9). We call this event the ascension. The word implies that heaven is 'above' and earth is 'below'. This was indeed the ancient view. 'Heaven' might be better described as 'being near to God'. Jesus left the earth to be near to his Father in heaven.

AND SITTETH ON THE RIGHT HAND OF GOD THE FATHER ALMIGHTY

The right hand of God is the place of honour. Jesus sits there because his work on earth is at an end. The reference is to the fact that the high priest always stood while officiating at the altar. Again, we are using words to describe something that cannot be described. What we are saying is that Jesus is now with God where he is able to act on our behalf, as the high priest acted for his people.

> The Saviour died, but rose again,
> Triumphant from the grave;
> And pleads our cause at God's right hand,
> Omnipotent to save.

FROM THENCE HE SHALL COME TO JUDGE THE QUICK AND THE DEAD

Christians believe that one day Jesus will return to this earth in glory. When or how he will do this, we are not told. Jesus simply said, 'Be on your guard, then, because you do not know the day or the hour' (*Matthew* 25:13). When he does come, however, it will be to pass judgment on everyone – on the 'quick' (ie those still living at that time) and the dead.

Jesus told several parables about Judgement Day. In one he says that we shall be judged according to how much love and compassion we have shown to those in need. In this parable (*Matthew* 25:31–46) we are told that we will be divided 'into two groups, just as a shepherd separates the sheep from the goats'. Among the sheep will be those who cared for the hungry and the thirsty and the homeless, and among the goats will be those who didn't.

ONE GOD, FATHER, SON AND HOLY SPIRIT

The Apostles' Creed says:

I BELIEVE IN THE HOLY GHOST

('Ghost' is an old word for 'Spirit')

The first mention of the Spirit is in the opening words of the Old Testament. 'The Spirit of God was moving over the face of the water' (*Genesis* 1:2). That same Spirit, we read in *Job* 33:4, 'made me and gave me life'.

As Jesus was coming up out of the water after his baptism 'he saw heaven opening and the Spirit coming down on him like a dove' (*Mark* 1:10). From earliest times the dove has been a symbol of the Holy Spirit, suggesting as it does love, gentleness and peace.

Like other things which have existed for centuries before they were discovered, eg electricity, nuclear power, etc the Holy Spirit was not fully understood or recognised until Jesus came. He prepared his disciples by telling them about the Holy Spirit and explaining that the Spirit would come to them after he had 'been raised to glory'. (*John* 7:39) On the day of Pentecost – a week after the ascension (see p 19) – the Holy Spirit came to the disciples as they were gathered together in Jerusalem.

THE HOLY SPIRIT IS A PERSON

Jesus did not speak about the Holy Spirit as 'it' but as 'he'. This is because the Holy Spirit is one of the three persons of the Trinity. As God has revealed himself as a Father and as the Son, so now he reveals himself in the Holy Spirit. The Holy Spirit is God in Jesus Christ alive and active in the world today. It is through the Holy Spirit that God makes himself known to us now.

ONE GOD, FATHER, SON AND HOLY SPIRIT

Jesus said, 'The wind blows wherever it wishes; you hear the sound it makes, but you do not know where it comes from or where it is going. It is like that with everyone who is born of the Spirit' *John* 3:8.

SPIRIT in Hebrew is *ruach* and in Greek *pneuma*. Both words mean 'breath' or 'wind'.

*   *   *   *   *

There is MYSTERY about the wind. You hear it but you cannot tell where it is going to blow next. So the Spirit sometimes touches our consciences and convicts us of sin. Or else he warms us with the breath of God's love and kindness. The wind of the Spirit can blow upon us at any time. We cannot tell what he will do.

The wind is its own MASTER. It blows where it wishes. All we can do is to react to it – protect ourselves against it or use it for our own purposes, eg to change the course of a yacht. When the Holy Spirit blows into our lives, we have either to turn away from him, ie cut ourselves off from God, or allow him to turn us in the direction he has chosen for us.

There is POWER in the wind. On the day of Pentecost 'there was a noise from the sky which sounded like a strong wind blowing' (*Acts* 2:2). It was the Holy Spirit fanning the flickering flames of the disciples' faith and firing them with new zeal and enthusiasm. On the day of Pentecost they discovered that God had given them the very power that Jesus had to work wonders and do miraculous things. It was the Holy Spirit acting in their lives.

ONE GOD, FATHER, SON AND HOLY SPIRIT

THE HOLY SPIRIT – from references in *John's Gospel*

The Holy Spirit is an AMBASSADOR. An ambassador is one who officially represents his country in another country. As he must always speak for his country, so the Holy Spirit always speaks for Jesus. Jesus said, 'He will not speak on his own authority, but he will speak of what he hears ... he will give me glory, because he will take what I say and tell it to you' (*John* 16:13, 14).

The Holy Spirit is a TEACHER. He explains Christ to us. If the Bible is our text-book of the life and teaching of Jesus, it is the Holy Spirit who puts the lesson across. Jesus said, 'The Holy Spirit ... will teach you everything and make you remember all that I have told you' (*John* 14:26).

The Holy Spirit is a HELPER. Jesus said, 'I will ask the Father, and he will give you another Helper, who will stay with you for ever' (*John* 14:16). The *AV* uses the word 'Comforter' in its original sense of 'someone who helps us to be brave'. The *NEB* translates it as 'Advocate', someone who will stand by us in a court of law. It is the same word as is used of a tug which comes alongside a large ship to help her navigate a difficult channel. The Holy Spirit helps us to face up to the problems of life and to deal with them as God would want us to do.

THE HOLY SPIRIT – from references in the *Book of Acts*.

On the day of Pentecost the Holy Spirit came like a strong wind and the believers 'saw what looked like tongues of fire which spread out and touched each person there. They were filled with the Holy Spirit and began to talk in other languages, as the Spirit enabled them to speak' (*Acts* 2:1–4).

Those who experienced the Holy Spirit in this way found themselves sharing in a new and exciting life together (*Acts* 2:42–45). They were able to heal the sick (*Acts* 3:1–10). They could speak with conviction about Jesus and the fact that he had risen from the dead (*Acts* 3:11–4:31). It was the Holy Spirit that had given them this new power.

THE CHRISTIAN YEAR

Many calendars and diaries show the special days and seasons that commemorate the various events from the birth of Jesus at Christmas to the coming of the Holy Spirit at Pentecost.

ADVENT means 'coming'. Advent is the four week period before Christmas. During it Christians prepare for the coming of Jesus but also for his second coming.

CHRISTMAS is the festival or mass commemorating the birth of Jesus on the 25th December.

EPIPHANY means 'appearance'. It is celebrated on the 6th January when traditionally the star which led the wise men to Jesus appeared in the sky.

LENT means 'lengthening', a Saxon name for the month of March when the days lengthened. It begins with ASH WEDNESDAY when ashes were sprinkled on the heads of penitent sinners. It continues for forty days. It also marks the period of Jesus' fasting in the wilderness and for Christians is often a time of self-denial.

PASSION SUNDAY, PALM SUNDAY, HOLY WEEK and GOOD FRIDAY. On the second last Sunday of Lent Christians remember the passion (or suffering) of Jesus. On the last Sunday they remember his procession into Jerusalem on the back of a donkey. Because this meant he was coming as a king the people waved palm branches and the day is known as Palm Sunday. This is the beginning of Holy Week which marks the last week in Jesus' life and ends with Good Friday when he was put to death on a cross.

EASTER DAY, the Sunday after Good Friday, is the day on which Christians remember the resurrection of Jesus. For the next forty days he appeared to his followers and this period ended with ASCENSION DAY when he ascended to be with his Father 'in heaven'.

PENTECOST was a Jewish festival held on the fiftieth (ie *Pentecoste)* day after Passover (see p 52) when Jesus ate the last supper with his disciples. On the day of Pentecost the Holy Spirit came to the believers gathered together in Jerusalem. It is better known as WHITSUNDAY because on that day converts to the new faith wore white after their baptism.

The Apostles' Creed says:

I BELIEVE IN THE FORGIVENESS OF SINS

A little girl who had been to church was asked afterwards what the minister had been saying. She thought hard and then said, 'He was talking about sin, and he was against it.' We are often equally vague about what we mean by 'sin' but we know that it is an evil thing that must be got rid of. Here are some things which the Bible says about sin.

Sin is 'crossing the line'

A motorist may not drive through traffic lights when they are at red. If he does, he has committed an offence. The Jews had certain lines that they were not allowed to cross. These were the rules and regulations laid down in their law book which includes the Ten Commandments (see *Exodus* 20). Jesus gave a further commandment: 'You shall love the Lord your God and your neighbour as yourself' (*Matthew* 22:37–40). To break any of these commandments is to transgress, to cross the line, to sin.

Sin is 'missing the mark'

In archery the aim is to get a bull's eye. To miss the mark is another word which the Bible uses for 'sin'. For Christians the bull's eye is to reach 'to the very height of Christ's full stature'. (*Ephesians* 4:12) to be as Christ is. If we fall short of this, we have sinned. We have missed the mark (see *Romans* 3:23 – *RSV*).

Sin can be in thought, word or action

The world judges us by our speech and our behaviour. God judges us – not just by the things that we say and do – but by the thoughts that we have in our hearts. That is why Jesus says it is as much an offence to nurse thoughts of anger against someone as to commit actual murder (see *Matthew* 5:21–22).

WHAT MAKES US SIN?

We sin because it is in our nature to sin. 'From the day of my birth I have been sinful' (*Psalm* 51:5). It began in the Garden of Eden with Adam and Eve. God gave them the freedom to eat the fruit of any tree except the one in the middle of the garden, 'the tree that gives knowledge of what is good and what is bad' (*Genesis* 2:17). If they ate the fruit of that tree, God said, they would die. The tempter (in the story, a snake) said to Eve, 'God said that, because he knows that when you eat it, you will be like God, and know what is good and what is bad' (*Genesis* 3:5). Eve gave in to the temptation and persuaded Adam also to eat of the fruit. They both wanted to be like God, indeed, to take over from God. This was the ORIGINAL SIN of mankind and we have all inherited it. Adam – his name means 'Man' – is representative of all of us. Whenever we give in to temptation, we are doing what Adam did when he committed the original sin.

WHAT HAPPENS WHEN WE SIN?

We lose the power to do good

Paul discovered how helpless he was when he tried to live a good life. 'Even though the desire to do good is in me, I am not able to do it... it is the sin that lives in me' (*Romans* 7:18, 20).

We lose the freedom to do good

'Everyone who sins is a slave of sin' (*John* 8:34). The more we sin, the more difficult it is for us not to sin. If we tell lies, or swear, or steal, we will get to the point where we can't stop doing these things. They will get the better of us. A little pet can turn into a wild animal and we become helpless in its grip.

We lose the favour of God

Sin is not just a moral failure, an unfortunate accident. Sin is an offence against God who is just and pure and holy. God cannot tolerate sin. If we sin, we can no longer enjoy the favour of God.

The first vow (second part)

DO YOU CONFESS JESUS CHRIST AS YOUR SAVIOUR AND LORD?

Losing the favour of God makes us feel guilty. When Adam and Eve ate the forbidden fruit 'they heard the Lord God walking in the garden, and they hid from him among the trees' (*Genesis* 3:8). They knew they had done wrong and they were afraid of the consequences. When God found them, he inflicted a punishment upon them. 'Because of what you have done ... you will have to work hard all your life to make the ground produce enough food for you' (*Genesis* 3:17). They were put out of the garden to cultivate the soil from which they had been formed. In the same way our sin banishes us from God, gives us a sense of guilt and makes us liable for punishment. How is it possible for us to get right again with God?

We can try to justify ourselves

This is what Adam tried to do. He did not blame himself for what he had done – he blamed Eve. 'The woman you put here with me gave me the fruit, and I ate it' (*Genesis* 3:11). In turn, Eve blamed the snake that had tempted her. Whenever we feel guilty because of something we have done, we always try to justify ourselves first, show that it is not our fault. But this does not get us right with God.

We can allow God to justify us

To get right with God, we must first acknowledge before him that we have sinned. 'If we confess our sins to God ... he will forgive us our sins and purify us from all our wrong-doing' (*1 John* 1:8). There is no alternative to confession. People used to think that by sacrificing an animal, they could make themselves right with God. The only sacrifice that pleases God is a change of heart, a willingness to confess sin and turn away from it. 'My sacrifice is a humble spirit, O God, you will not reject a humble and repentant heart' (*Psalm* 52:17). By doing this we are no longer justifying ourselves; we are allowing God to justify us. It is only possible of course, because of what Jesus has done. He has paid the price of our sin. He has received the punishment that we should have received. But it allows us to go free, to be justified and to be accepted by God.

'THERE WAS ONCE A MAN WHO HAD TWO SONS: THE YOUNGER ONE SAID TO HIM, FATHER, GIVE ME MY SHARE OF THE PROPERTY NOW...HE SOLD HIS PART AND LEFT HOME WITH THE MONEY. HE WENT TO A COUNTRY FAR AWAY WHERE HE WASTED HIS MONEY IN RECKLESS LIVING.

HE SPENT EVERYTHING HE HAD...NO ONE GAVE HIM ANYTHING TO EAT...AT LAST HE CAME TO HIS SENSES AND SAID, I WILL GET UP AND GO TO MY FATHER...'

Luke 15:11 ff.

The parable of the prodigal son is an illustration of the way in which God can put right a broken relationship. Let us put ourselves in the position of the son who went away.

(1) **He was sick of home**

The son thought he would be happier away from home where his father would have no authority over him. Often we think we will be happier if we can go where we will not be subject to the authority of our heavenly Father.

(2) **He was home-sick**

In that far away country the son didn't find life as wonderful as he expected. He enjoyed it until the money ran out. Hard times made him do a lot of soul-searching. 'He came to his senses', and decided that he would go back to his father and confess that he had made a mess of things. This change of heart was his 'conversion'. In real life it means turning away from self and turning towards God who is our heavenly Father.

(3) **He was home**

The son had no idea about what kind of reception he would get when he got back home. He expected to have to live in the servants' quarters. But instead 'he was still a long way off from home when his father saw him; his heart was filled with pity, and he ran, threw his arms round his son, and kissed him' (*Luke* 15:20). His father wanted to take him right back into the family. God too comes looking for us when we are repentant and welcomes us back into his home. And thus a broken relationship is restored.

A TALE ABOUT A COURT CASE

Two former school friends met in unusual circumstances. One had become an eminent judge; the other, a notorious criminal. One day the latter found himself in court with his friend seated on the bench. Duly relieved, he contented himself with the thought that his friend would let him off lightly. He was wrong. The judge fined him as severely as the law would allow. The prisoner looked bewildered until he saw his friend come down into the court, take off his wig and gown, and write out a cheque for the amount. Justice demanded that the judge should punish his friend but love prompted him to pay the fine himself.

GOD IS JUST

'Justice' or 'righteousness' are familiar biblical words. Basically they mean 'that which is as it should be'. When we say that God is just, we mean that he has absolute standards of right and wrong, and that he demands such standards of his people. That is why in the Bible God is always seen as opposed to any kind of evil, eg injustice or oppression, but ready always to uphold what is right. 'He raises the humble, but crushes the wicked to the ground' (*Psalm* 147:6).

GOD IS LOVING

If Amos was the prophet who spoke principally about God's justice, Hosea was the prophet who spoke principally about his love. Amos told of how God was angry with the man who exploited his neighbour (*Amos* 5:7ff). Hosea told of how God forgave people like the prophet's own wife who had been unfaithful to him (*Hosea* 2:2ff). In his own life and teaching Jesus showed that while God condemns sin, he still loves the sinner and desires above all things that he should be forgiven. Jesus came to 'share our sin in order that in union with him we might share the righteousness of God' (*2 Corinthians* 5:21).

24

We know that Jesus is SAVIOUR

(a) because of his *teaching*. Read the three parables in *Luke* 15 – the lost sheep, the lost coin, the lost son.

(b) because of his *life and example*. Jesus spent his whole time searching for those who were lost. Read the story in *Luke* 19:1–6 of Zacchaeus, the mean little tax-collector whom Jesus found and turned into a new person. 'The Son of Man came to seek and to save the lost.'

(c) because of his *death*. The cross showed how far God was prepared to go to forgive those who had wronged him. To those who crucified him, Jesus said, 'Forgive them, Father! They don't know what they are doing' (*Luke* 23:34).

His death was voluntary

Jesus was never the victim of those who wanted to kill him. He chose to die. 'No one takes my life away from me. I give it up of my own free will' (*John* 10:18).

His death was vicarious

This meant that Jesus did not die for his own sake but for the sake of those whom he wanted to save. 'The greatest love a person can have for his friends is to give his life for them' (*John* 15:13).

We know that Jesus is LORD

(a) because through his death he has saved us from our sins. Anyone who has saved us, say from drowning, would have a claim on our lives. We would owe to that person a deep debt of gratitude. In the same way we owe a debt of loyalty and devotion to Jesus who died for us but rose again to be with us always.

(b) because by his rising again he has defeated death and shown that sin and evil no longer have any hold over him. That is why 'God gave him the name that is greater than any other name' and why Christians 'proclaim that Jesus Christ is Lord'. (*Philippians* 2:10, 11).

B

ON WHAT IT MEANS TO BE A CHRISTIAN

We may be 'Christian' by tradition or upbringing but in the biblical sense a Christian is a person who has a special relationship to Christ. How does one get this? There is an African proverb which says, 'When one would climb a tree, one begins from the bottom and not from the top.' To be a Christian we must start where we are and take a look at Jesus.

(1) If you see Jesus as the one who sums up for you all that you would like to be as a person, that is a good starting-point. Peter wanted to be like Jesus but when he looked at him he felt he just wasn't good enough. 'Go away from me, Lord', he said, 'for I am a sinful man' (*Luke* 5:8).

(2) You can't become like Jesus simply by trying to live like him. You have first got to get rid of the sin in your life. Paul said that what hindered him in living a good life was 'the sin that lives in me' (*Romans* 7:20). Acknowledge your sin before God, be sorry for it and ask him to forgive you. God will help you in this. He 'is trying to lead you to repent' (*Romans* 2:4).

(3) When you have repented, believe that God has forgiven you your sins and forgotten about them. 'I will forgive their sins and will no longer remember their wrongs' (*Hebrews* 8:12). Don't try to recall your sins but deliberately turn away from them. 'Do those things that will show you have turned from your sins' (*Luke* 3:8). Begin to live as a Christian.

(4) Don't try to do this on your own. As a Christian you will still meet with temptation. You will often be encouraged to go back to the old way of life. Resist this temptation. Remember that Jesus who has forgiven you your sins is standing by you. His Holy Spirit is there to help you to live as a Christian.

(5) You now have a new direction for your life. You are still far from being as Christ is but you are moving towards it. 'I do not claim that I have already become perfect', said Paul when he became a Christian, 'but I run straight towards the goal in order to win the prize, which is God's call through Christ Jesus to the life above' (*Philippians* 3:12, 14).

ON WHAT IT IS LIKE TO BE A CHRISTIAN

In the New Testament there are two descriptions of what Christians – or Christ folk – are like.

A Christian is someone in whom Christ lives

Paul says, 'I have been put to death with Christ on his cross, so that it is no longer I who live but it is Christ who lives in me' (*Galatians* 2:20). 'I' is the central letter of 'sin'. In a non-Christian life the 'I' predominates. For a Christian the 'I' has been crucified with Christ. Sin is no more. Christ takes the place of sin in the Christian's life.

Someone has said that when a man becomes a Christian, Christ becomes his boss! It is like a shop that comes 'under new management'. It is the same shop as before but there is a different person in charge. When someone becomes a Christian he or she is the same individual as before but now Christ is in charge.

A Christian is someone who lives in Christ

Paul says, 'When anyone is joined to Christ [or, is in Christ–*RSV*], he is a new being; the old has gone, the new has come' (*2 Corinthians* 5:17). Jesus once said to a man, 'You must be born again' (*John* 2:7). He didn't mean it literally – as the man discovered. He meant that being a Christian is similar to being born again, seeing the world, as it were, for the first time but now as with the eyes of Christ. For the Christian, therefore, even ordinary things have a new look. This is how G W Robinson, the hymn-writer, described it:

> Heaven above is softer blue,
>   Earth around is sweeter green;
> Something lives in every hue,
>   Christless eyes have never seen.
> Birds with gladder songs o'erflow,
>   Flowers with deeper beauties shine,
> Since I know, as now I know,
>   I am His, and He is mine.

ON WHAT IS INVOLVED IN BEING A CHRISTIAN

Becoming a Christian is only the beginning of a long journey. Often the way ahead is harder than the way behind. In the rest of this book we shall be examining what it means to be a Christian in terms of our everyday life. Here is a summary of the remaining vows which refer to this and at which we shall be looking in some detail.

WE MUST JOIN REGULARLY WITH OUR FELLOW CHRISTIANS IN WORSHIP ON THE LORD'S DAY

Regular worship with others and coming to church on a Sunday is not something which Christians do out of a sense of duty but because they enjoy it. In Psalm 122:1 the writer says, 'I was glad when they said to me, Let us go to the Lord's house.'

WE MUST BE FAITHFUL IN READING THE BIBLE, AND IN PRAYER

The Bible is God's word. He speaks to us from it. As we read the Bible 'listening for his voice', we may find a verse that just expresses our feelings or answers our needs at that particular moment. This is God speaking to us. He also speaks to us – and we can talk to him – through prayer. The Bible and prayer are two channels through which we can keep in touch with God. It is important that we keep these channels open.

WE MUST GIVE OF OUR TIME, OUR TALENTS AND OUR MONEY FOR THE CHURCH'S WORK IN THE WORLD

We owe everything to God – the hours of each day, our skills and abilities, the money that we earn or that is given to us. He asks that we use these things to further the work of his Church throughout the world.

WE MUST CONFESS CHRIST BEFORE MEN, SERVE HIM IN OUR DAILY WORK AND WALK IN HIS WAYS ALL THE DAYS OF OUR LIFE

We must be willing to commend Christ to others, to dedicate our work-a-day life to him and to walk in the Christian way all through our lives.

28

ON WHAT IT MEANS TO BE A MEMBER OF THE CHURCH

Being a Christian makes you a member of the family of Christ. In practice you must live this out within the family of a particular Christian congregation. Your local church is where you will find this family. Membership of the Church does not mean simply having your name on a congregational roll. It means sharing in the life of the Christian family and there are different stages at which you can be a member of it.

BAPTISMAL MEMBERSHIP

Baptism is the mark of entry into the Church, into the Christian family (see also pp 48 ff). It has been the same from the earliest times. Some are baptised in infancy; others are baptised as believers. If you were baptised as a baby, you may have a certificate of your baptism or your birth certificate may have been endorsed by the minister who baptised you. If you have not been baptised before, you can be baptised now. At whatever point it is given, baptism is the outward sign that you have been received into membership of the Church.

ADHERENT MEMBERSHIP

An adherent (compare 'adhesive') is one who 'sticks' to the Church. Technically an adherent is one who has been baptised, who practises as a Christian but who is not a communicant member. There are many such adherents in the churches in the Highlands and Islands of Scotland. They are good Christians but they do not feel worthy to receive communion. This, however, is to misunderstand what communion is for.

COMMUNICANT MEMBERSHIP

A communicant member is one who is in full communion with Christ and with his Church. Usually he first receives instruction in the Christian faith and then publicly acknowledges Jesus Christ as his Lord and Saviour. In this he is not showing himself worthy but is accepting God's forgiveness for his sins. Before he actually receives communion he confirms his baptism at a special service where he takes the vows that are outlined on p 3.

ON CHRISTIAN WORSHIP

The second vow

DO YOU PROMISE TO JOIN REGULARLY WITH YOUR FELLOW CHRISTIANS IN WORSHIP ON THE LORD'S DAY?

Why should we go to church?

If we are Christians we will want to go to church on a Sunday and worship with other Christians. Worship is our response to the God who created us.

> Come, let us bow down and worship him,
> Let us kneel before the Lord, our Maker.
>> He is our God;
>> We are the people he cares for,
>> the flock for which he provides.
>
> Psalm 95

We can, of course, worship God on our own but as Christians we belong to a family and the church is the place where the family can worship together.

What should we do in church?

(a) We should remember that we are in the presence of the risen Christ. We should think of him first. A friend of Leonardo da Vinci, admiring his unfinished painting of the last supper, remarked on the loveliness of the two silver cups. Immediately the artist took his brush and painted them out. 'It is not the cups I want you to see', he said, 'it's the face of Jesus!' Everything in church – the words, the music, the architecture, the atmosphere – is to help us 'to see Jesus' (*John* 12:21), and so to worship him.

(b) We should remember that we are in the presence of God's people. A congregation, whatever its size, is a fellowship of people from all kinds of backgrounds who are united in Christ. At a church service, however, we also have a 'large crowd of witnesses round us' (*Hebrews* 12:1), all those who have died believing in Jesus and who are never far from us in the fellowship of prayer.

ON CHRISTIAN WORSHIP

Here are some things to think about on the subject of Christian worship.

*   *   *   *   *

R W Emerson, the American poet, once said, 'I have a little flower in my heart called Reverence, and I like to water it once a week.' Is this why people today come to church on a Sunday? Is it enough to worship God once a week?

*   *   *   *   *

How does your church look on a Sunday? Like this?

THIS .... IS THE .. WAY .... THE CHURCH LOOKS ..... WHEN .... IT IS .. HALF EMPTY

Or like this?

THISISTHEWAYTHECHURCHWOULDLOOKIFEVERYONECAMEEVERYWEEK

Why do people prefer to worship in a church that is fairly full?

*   *   *   *   *

What is the most important thing for you in a church service? The people? The feeling of fellowship? The hymns? The music? The readings? The prayers? The sermon? The message? The children's part? The offering? Is any one part of the service more important than another?

Why is it easier to worship God in a church than in most other places? Why do some people say that it is not necessary to come to church to worship God?

*   *   *   *   *

How meaningful for you is the Sunday worship in your own church? What changes would you like to see that would make the services more meaningful? Remember that a minister has to plan a service for all who are likely to come to it – for children and teenagers, for the middle-aged and the elderly, for people alone and for people in families.

WHAT IS THE CHURCH?

The Apostles' Creed says:

I BELIEVE IN THE HOLY, CATHOLIC CHURCH

Holy = set apart for a sacred or religious use.
Catholic = universal, embracing all Christians.
Church = ?

Here are some possible meanings of the word 'church'. Try to distinguish between them.

(1) The Church is wherever God's people are praising,
      Singing their thanks for joy on this day,
  The Church is wherever disciples of Jesus
      Remember his story and walk in his way.

  The Church is wherever God's people are helping,
      Caring for neighbours in sickness and need;
  The Church is wherever God's people are sharing
      The words of the Bible in gift and in deed.
                              Carol Rose Ikeler

(2) I am a member of St Andrews Church.

(3) We are all going to church this morning.

(4) My church is the one with the red spire at the top of the hill.

(5) The Church does not approve of gambling.

(6) I am Church of Scotland but my friend is a Baptist.

(7) The Church is to be found all over the world.

(8) The Church's one foundation is Jesus Christ her Lord.

The word CHURCH comes from the Greek *kuriakon* which means 'belonging to the Lord'. The Church did not begin with the disciples but with Jesus himself. He founded it for the purpose of carrying on his work and the Church, therefore, belongs to him.

The Church is not just a building, a place of worship, a religious denomination, an institution. It is first and foremost people – God's people. 'You are a chosen race, the king's priests, the holy nation, God's own people' (*1 Peter* 2:9). These names were originally given to the Israelites, God's chosen race, but now they refer to the Church. These people, because of their special relationship to Christ, got the nickname 'Christian' (*Acts* 11:26) which meant 'Christ folk'. Here are some descriptions of the Church as the people of God.

The flock of God
(*1 Peter* 5:2–3)

Jesus referred to himself as 'the good shepherd' who cares for his flock (*John* 10:7 ff). We have all 'strayed like sheep' (*Isaiah* 53:6), but he has gone out to look for us and to bring us back into the fold.

The family in the faith
(*Galatians* 6:10)

The *NEB* refers to 'the household of faith'. All who belong to the royal household are personally appointed by the Queen. It is Jesus who selects those who are to belong to the household of faith. 'You did not choose me; I chose you and appointed you' (*John* 15:16).

God's building
(*1 Corinthians* 3:9)

Peter said, 'Come as living stones, and let yourselves be used in building the spiritual temple' (*1 Peter* 2:5). Asked by a visitor where the walls of Sparta were, the King pointed to his bodyguard of soldiers. 'These are the walls of Sparta', he said, 'and everyone of them a brick.'

The body of Christ
(*Romans* 12:4–5)

In *1 Corinthians* 12:27 Paul says, 'All of you are Christ's body, and each of you is a part of it.' As a leg or an eye cannot function apart from the body, so neither can the individual Christian unless he or she is part of the Church which is 'the body of Christ'.

HOW THE CHURCH BEGAN

The Church began with Jesus himself. He chose twelve men to be his disciples. They were to learn from him (a disciple was a learner) in order to carry on his work. He called them 'the salt of the earth' (*Matthew* 5:13, *AV*) and 'the light of the world' (*Matthew* 5:14, *AV*). Here are their names:

THE DISCIPLES

Simon Peter	Andrew	James	John
Philip	Bartholomew	Matthew	Thomas
James, son of Alphaeus		Simon, the Zealot	
Judas, son of James		Judas Iscariot	

After they had been with him for some time Jesus asked them if they knew who he really was. It was Simon Peter who spoke up. 'You are the Messiah, the Son of the living God.' Jesus said he would found his Church on people with a faith like that of Peter. 'You are a rock', he said to him, 'and on this rock foundation I will build my church, and not even death will ever be able to overcome it' (*Matthew* 16:16, 18).

In Jesus' day there was already a church–the Jewish Church–but it had become so rigid in its structure that the 'new wine' (*Matthew* 9:17) of Jesus' teaching just could not be contained within it. That was why Jesus had to found a new church based upon faith in him. Those who belonged to it were to walk in his ways (the Christians were sometimes called 'the People of the Way') and to tell others about him. In this task they would not be alone. He would help them. 'You will be filled with power when the Holy Spirit comes upon you...' (*Acts* 2:8).

Jesus explained to his disciples that the Holy Spirit would only come after he had left them. 'It is better for you that I go away', he said, 'because if I do not go, the Helper will not come to you' (*John* 16:7). The Holy Spirit came, in fact, when 'all the believers were gathered together in one place' (*Acts* 2:1) on the Day of Pentecost. Now they knew that Jesus' power would be available to them 'to the end of the age' (*Matthew* 28:20). This was the birth-day of the Christian Church. (See also p 18.)

...AND A STORY FROM ITS EARLY DAYS

Read this account of an incident in the life of the Church in Jerusalem from *Acts* 3:1–9

Peter and John are now Christians but they continue their Jewish practice of going to the Temple at the set times for prayer. On their way to worship God one day they are stopped by a man who has been a cripple all his life and who is brought each day to the entrance of the Temple to beg for money. Peter explains that he has no money – the apostles pooled all their money so that none of them was ever in need – but he offers the cripple something better, the power to walk again.

He says to the man, 'In the name of Jesus Christ of Nazareth, I order you to get up and walk.' He helps him up and the man's feet and ankles become strong again. He is no longer a cripple and goes 'into the Temple with them, walking and jumping and praising God.' It is the first healing miracle by one of the apostles.

Some thoughts for our own situation...

(a) The Christians in Jerusalem continued to meet in the Temple for worship. In his lifetime Jesus went regularly to synagogue. Should coming to church on a Sunday be a habit we acquire or something we do just when we feel like it?

(b) The miracle took place while Peter and John were on their way to worship God. Were they at that time expecting great things from God? When we go to church, do we expect God to do great things for us?

(c) The cripple, now cured, was able to walk into the Temple with Peter and John, and give thanks to God. Do we join others at church when we feel particularly grateful?

HOW THE CHURCH DEVELOPED

The first Church was that which was founded in Jerusalem. Gradually missionaries took the message of Jesus to other places. One of them, Paul, travelled widely and eventually brought the gospel to Rome, the capital of the greatest empire in the world (*Acts* 28:26–30).

The Church grew in strength but because it recognised God's authority before that of the Roman Emperor, it soon came into conflict with the state. Successive emperors persecuted the Christians but, as Tertullian, a convert to the faith, said, 'The blood of the martyrs became the seed of the Church.'

In 312 the Emperor Constantine on his way to battle saw a cross in the sky and the words 'By this conquer!' He ordered a cross to be drawn on the shields of all his soldiers and he won the battle. From that time he allowed Christians full freedom of worship.

The Church in Rome itself was now given every support by the Emperor and in time the Bishop of Rome became the most important of all the bishops. From the fourth century he was known as the 'Pope' and ruled over the whole of the Church.

As the Church expanded still further, two main traditions developed. In the West the church with its centre in Rome became known as the '(Roman) Catholic Church' while in the East the church with its centre in Constantinople (named after Constantine but now called Istanbul) became known as the '(Eastern) Orthodox Church'. This division still exists today.

In 1073 Hildebrande became Pope and for the next four centuries the Church in Rome became the most powerful institution in the West. Power, however, can be self-destructive. The Church became rich and corrupt. Travelling preachers known as friars called for a return to the simple life and the simple gospel. John Wycliffe, a poor parson, translated the Bible into English. Ordinary people could now read it and they realised that the Church had departed from the teaching of the scriptures.

A Reformation movement began with Martin Luther in Germany, with John Calvin in Switzerland and with John Knox in Scotland. By the sixteenth century the Western Church had split into the Roman Catholic Church and the Reformed or Protestant (called after the people who had protested) churches.

GROWTH OF THE CHURCH IN SCOTLAND

AD

400   Ninian with some monks arrived from France at Whithorn on the Solway Firth and built his 'little white house'.

563   Columba landed on Iona from Ireland and founded a monastery (a community of monks) on the island.

635   Aidan, a member of this community, introduced the Celtic Church (as it was called) to the people of Northumbria. He built a church on Lindisfarne (Holy Island).

1069   Margaret, a Saxon princess, came to Dunfermline and married Malcolm Canmore, King of Scotland. She was a Christian, and greatly influenced the Scots. Their third son, David I, built abbeys at Dryburgh, Kelso and Melrose.

1526   Tyndale's English translation of the Bible was smuggled into Leith. Scots now able to read the Bible for themselves for the first time realised that the church was in need of reform. The Reformers – men like Patrick Hamilton, George Wishart and John Knox – met a great deal of opposition from the established church in Scotland.

1547   Knox, formerly a priest, was appointed as preacher at St Andrews. The French fleet attacked the port, took Knox prisoner and made him a

1559   galley-slave. He returned to Scotland and preached against Rome from the pulpit of St John's Kirk in Perth. After the service the congregation destroyed every Roman Catholic image in the town.

1561   Mary, Queen of Scots, defender of the Roman Catholic Faith, landed in Leith from France. She ordered Mass to be said at Holyrood. Knox preached against it. Her son, James VI – later James I of England – tried to establish episcopacy in Scotland. Andrew Melville, however,

1581   reminded him that though he was King of Scotland, he was not sovereign of Christ's realm and he produced a Book of Discipline in which he argued for presbyterian government in the Scottish church.

1638   James's son, Charles I, ordered the English (Episcopal) Service Book to be used in all churches in Scotland. Jenny Geddes protested by throwing a stool at the preacher in St Giles Cathedral in Edinburgh and this eventually led to the signing of the National Covenant which aimed at restoring 'the purity and liberty of the Gospel'.

The church is called ROMAN because it is centred in Rome. CATHOLIC means 'universal, embracing all Christians' (see p 32).

Origin of the Roman Catholic Church

Roman Catholics regard Peter as the first Bishop of Rome and claim that Jesus gave him a special personal authority when he said to him, 'Peter! You are a rock, and on this rock foundation I will build my church' (*Matthew* 16:18). Protestants hold the view that Jesus was referring here, not to Peter as an individual, but to Peter as one who had been able to say to him, 'You are the Messiah, the Son of the living God' (*Matthew* 16:16). On this confession of faith, he said, he would build his Church.

Government of the Roman Catholic Church

The church is governed by a council or college of cardinals headed by the Pope (or Papa, Father), the name given to the Bishop of Rome. Below him are the other bishops, the successors of the apostles, and priests. Some priests, honoured by the Pope, are addressed as 'Monsignor'. Monks, friars and nuns are members of religious orders who have taken vows of poverty, chastity and obedience to a rule.

Teaching of the Roman Catholic Church

The church was founded by Jesus Christ, the Son of God and it will last till the end of time. It teaches with Christ's authority and is protected from error. It observes seven sacraments, the chief of which is baptism. The Pope, as the successor of Peter, is regarded as Christ's vicar or representative on earth. His word is authoritative on all matters of church doctrine and Christian behaviour. The church's beliefs are based on the Apostles' and Nicene Creeds, on the Bible including the Apocrypha (see p 59) and on the tradition of the church itself.

THE REFORMED OR PROTESTANT CHURCHES

At the Reformation there was a break away from the traditions of the medieval church centred in Rome. Turning to the scriptures for their authority, the Reformed churches interpreted these according to their own understanding and so formed a variety of denominations, eg Baptists, Congregationalists, Episcopalians, Methodists, Presbyterians, etc. The differences were largely over the question of how the church should be governed. Since 1910 there has been an ECUMENICAL (*'Oikou Mene'* = 'The Inhabited World') MOVEMENT which seeks to bring about a closer understanding between the denominations. Today there is close co-operation between most of the reformed  churches and many shared activities with the Roman Catholic Church. Below are listed some of the better known denominations within the Reformed or Protestant tradition.

BAPTIST CHURCH

This Church teaches that baptism should be given only to believers and not to infants. Baptism is generally done by immersion in a pool of water. Baptists stress the need for an evangelical faith and among their followers is Billy Graham, the evangelist. John Bunyan and William Carey, the first Christian missionary to India, were also Baptists.

CONGREGATIONAL CHURCH

Congregationalists have a similar evangelical emphasis and follow the pattern of the early Christians who met together for worship in the way that suited them best. Each congregation of this church may determine the form of worship which it wishes to use. The Church Meeting is the central gathering. The Pilgrim Fathers who went to America in the *Mayflower* were Congregationalists.

CHRISTIAN BRETHREN

These are groups of Christian lay people who form themselves into a brotherhood and do not have ordained ministers. At first they were known as Plymouth Brethren but today many call themselves Evangelical Churches. They stress the authority of the scriptures and have communion – the breaking of bread – every Sunday. Some groups are open and welcome other Christians. Others are known as closed or exclusive brethren.

THE REFORMED OR PROTESTANT CHURCHES

EPISCOPAL CHURCH

'Episcopal' means 'government by bishops'. This church has a three-fold ministry of bishops, priests and deacons. The Episcopal Church in Scotland is in full communion with the state or established Church of England. In Scotland the church was disestablished in 1689.

When the worldwide Anglican communion – churches that follow the same tradition as the Church of England – has a conference of its bishops, it is presided over by the Archbishop of Canterbury. The Episcopal Church in Scotland has no archbishop but its leading bishop is called the Primus. He presides over the Episcopal Synod, the supreme court of appeal for the church. Below this are diocesan synods administering the affairs of each diocese, the name of the area over which a bishop has jurisdiction. The financial affairs of the church are handled by the Representative Church Council and, lower down, by the Diocesan Council and the Vestry.

A cathedral where the Bishop has his throne or seat (Latin, *cathedra*) is run by a Chapter consisting of the Bishop, the Dean who acts for him in his absence, the Provost who is the rector or minister of the cathedral, and the canons who act in an advisory capacity. The priest of a local church is called the Rector.

The central act of the church is holy communion or the eucharist. The Book of Common Prayer used by the Scottish church is different from that used by the Church of England, but both provide a service book which allows the congregation to participate actively in the worship.

METHODIST CHURCH

This church was founded by John Wesley and his brother, Charles, who together formed a 'holy club' in 1729 and decided to live methodically according to the rules laid down in the Bible. Both brothers had a convincing religious experience – John felt his heart 'strangely warmed' when visiting a church in Aldersgate in London – and they brought a warm-hearted Christianity to people all over England. John was the preacher; Charles was the hymn-writer. They travelled widely, mainly on horseback and spoke in particular to the poor and the socially deprived. 'The world is my parish', said John Wesley. Methodist preachers – not all are ordained ministers – still travel on circuit and only remain in any one church for a limited number of years.

CHURCH OF SCOTLAND

There has been a church in Scotland since Celtic times. Since 1690 the established church in the country has been Presbyterian. There have been several subsequent breakaways, notably at the Disruption in 1843 when the Free Church of Scotland was formed. One of the controversies was over the right of congregations to choose their own minister. In 1929 there was a union of all the main Presbyterian churches in Scotland and only a few continued to stay out (see below). The Church of Scotland today is the national church in Scotland and in common with other Presbyterian churches it has as its emblem the burning bush (see *Exodus* 3:2).

Other Presbyterian churches in Scotland
(a) Reformed Presbyterian Church which holds rigidly to the principles of the National Covenant of 1638.
(b) Free Church – sometimes known as the Wee Frees – which 'went out' in 1843 and stayed out of any later unions.
(c) Free Presbyterian Church, a splinter group from the Free Church and which claims to be the true Church of Scotland.
(d) United Free Church (Continuing), a union of Free churches which did not 'come in' at the 1929 Union.

Teaching of the Church of Scotland
It recognises the Old and New Testaments as the supreme rule of faith and life. Its General Assembly may formulate its own doctrines provided these are 'in agreement with the Word of God' and do not conflict with the fundamentals of the Christian faith.

Government of the Church of Scotland
Presbyterian, which means government by presbyters or elders. A minister is a teaching – as opposed to a ruling – elder, and no minister enjoys a status above that of another minister. Government is through courts from the General Assembly down to the Presbytery and Kirk Session. In each court except the Kirk Session (which is the court of a congregation) there is an equal number of ministers and elders. The chairman of each court is known as the moderator. The General Assembly appoints annually its own Moderator and its meetings are attended by the Queen or her personal representative, the Lord High Commissioner.

JUDAISM

The most important of these, from our point of view, is the Jewish religion. Jesus was a Jew. Christianity, therefore, has a Jewish background. The religion is known as Judaism from Judah, the land which God promised to Abraham and to the nation of which he was to be the founder (see *Genesis* 12:1–3). The Jews thus came to be God's chosen race. 'I will be your God, and you will be my people' (*Leviticus* 26:12).

In Abraham's time the Jews were called the Hebrews because Abraham belonged to the Habiru tribe. Abraham's son was Isaac and his grandson was Jacob, also known as Israel. Gradually the Hebrew people were referred to as the Israelites or the children of Israel. In New Testament times they are called the Jews.

The holy books

The Old Testament, particularly the first five books, known as the *Pentateuch*, the *Torah* or the Law. They include the Ten Commandments. Another book, the *Talmud*, is a collection of rules relating the *Torah* to situations of everyday life.

The holy places

The holy place was the Temple in Jerusalem. Jews now worship in synagogues. Men and women separate on entering. At any service there must be ten male Jews present. The rabbi, the local Jewish teacher, reads and explains the scriptures which are in scroll form (see *Luke* 4:16–30 for an example of Jesus reading the scriptures).

The holy days

The sabbath is from sunset on Friday to sunset on Saturday. To mark it candles are lit. Men go to synagogue on the Friday evening and the whole family goes on the sabbath. Other holy days are *Rosh Hashana* (New Year) and *Yom Kippur* (Day of Atonement).

The holy feasts or festivals

All are linked with the harvest. They are the Passover (barley), Pentecost (wheat) and Tabernacles (grapes, olives).

THE NON-CHRISTIAN RELIGIONS

A growing interest in meditation and mysticism has turned many people to Eastern religion and philosophy. The gurus teach that the aim of life is to become one with the universe. This gives meaning to such Hindu sects and organisations as the Divine Light Mission, the Hare Krishna Movement and Transcendental Meditation. Here we can only look at the three major Eastern religions.

HINDUISM is a mixture of faiths. Its sacred books are called the *Vedas*. Time is a cycle and each soul can be reincarnated in a different form in a future existence. This depends upon the kind of life each person lives. There is a strict caste or class system with Brahmins at the top and outcastes or untouchables at the bottom. A Hindu passes through four stages of life by way of yoga, ie yoking the mind to God. He may choose a god, eg Vishna or Shiva, as his patron. The River Ganges is sacred to the Hindu as are certain animals and trees.

BUDDHISM is a title, not a name. Buddha was 'the Enlightened One'. His real name was Gautama. He was brought up in luxury but as a young man he saw suffering that made him want to help his fellow men and discover the true meaning of life. Sitting under a fig tree he found enlightenment. Suffering, he said, is caused by desire. Get rid of desire by following certain 'right' principles and you will get rid of suffering. To do this properly means becoming a monk. The aim of life is to reach Nirvana, the state of perfect peace, and this can only be done by performing good deeds. Buddha was not a god but a teacher.

ISLAM was the name which Mohammed gave to the religion which he formed. The word means 'submission to God'. Mohammed was born in Mecca in AD 570. The Koran, the Moslem's holy book, is said to have been recited to Mohammed by Gabriel from an original copy in heaven. It lays down five duties for all Moslems (those who practise Islam): recite the creed, pray five times a day, give alms to help the poor, fast during Ramadan – the month when the Koran was given to Mohammed – and make a pilgrimage to Mecca.

THE CULTS

Cults are religious groups which make use of the Bible but either add to it or misinterpret its teaching. They usually regard Jesus as someone less than the Son of God. By their enthusiasm they often win over lapsed members of the mainstream churches.

JEHOVAH'S WITNESSES

They get their name from a translation of *Isaiah* 43:22: 'Ye are my witnesses, saith Jehovah.' Jesus, they say, was not the incarnation of God but was a kind of in-between being. The movement was founded by Charles Russell in 1881. Its official publication is *The Watch Tower*. Jehovah's Witnesses call their churches 'Kingdom Halls'. They do regular visiting offering Bible courses and other literature.

CHURCH OF JESUS CHRIST OF LATTER DAY SAINTS (MORMONS)

Their principal scripture is the *Book of Mormon* – supposedly a translation from golden plates dug up on a hillside – and said by them to be more accurate in translation than the Bible. Joseph Smith (1805–1844), the founder of their church, was able to 'translate' the writing on the plates by wearing special glasses. They do not accept Jesus as the full and final revelation of God. Smith and his successors in office claim to have had further revelations. Mormons call themselves Latter Day Saints and young missionaries will give up to two years to spread their 'eternal gospel'.

CHURCH OF CHRIST, SCIENTIST (CHRISTIAN SCIENTISTS)

This church was founded by Mary Baker Eddy in 1866. She taught that because God is good, everything evil – sickness, pain, and death – do not exist in God's world but are only in the mind. The cure is to have the Christ Spirit which is the source of right thinking. All this is taught in the founder's commentary *Science and Health with Key to the Scriptures* which can be read in a Christian Science reading room. Christianity does not teach that suffering is an illusion. It is a fact of life which is contrary to God's will, but Christ has come to take away suffering or to help sufferers to endure it (see *2 Corinthians* 12:7–10).

UNIFICATION CHURCH (MOONISM)

Founded in 1936 by a Korean called Sun Myung Moon. He claims to be a kind of messiah in whom all the religions of the world will be united. Jesus said, 'When I am lifted up from the earth, I will draw everyone to me' (*John* 12:32). The Moonies, as they are called, have a highly organised missionary programme.

The occult or the psychic is the attempt of the mind to come into direct contact with the supernatural or spirit world. Here are some of the familiar forms of it.

SPIRITISM or SPIRITUALISM

Spiritualism is the religion based on Spiritism. It is the practice of communicating with the dead with the help of a spirit-guide or medium. Spiritualists have churches and may claim to be Christians. Spiritists are atheists. Christians do not believe that after death their spirits continue to exist as in this life; they live in a new kind of world altogether for they are 'with Christ' (*Philippians* 1:23).

FUTURE TELLING or FORTUNE TELLING

This is based on the belief that the future is already planned and that we can discover what this is by means of horoscopes, crystal balls, ouija boards, etc. Man, however, has free will and therefore has a hand in determining the future. The Christian believes that God has a purpose for every man's life and that he 'works for good with those who love him' (*Romans* 8:28). We should simply entrust the future to God.

HYPNOTISM, MIND EXPANSION, TRANSCENDENTAL MEDITATION, YOGA

These practices mostly originate in Eastern religion and are an attempt to escape from the real world or to commune with the spirit world. Under their influence the mind becomes passive and open to outside suggestions which may come from the devil. 'Satan can disguise himself to look like an angel of light' (*2 Corinthians* 11:14). Christianity does not offer an escape from life but communion with Christ who can only influence us for good.

SORCERY, BLACK MAGIC, WITCHCRAFT

This is another evil practice in which some people dabble. Usually it is because they hope by this means to get wealth or power or some other material advantage. In fact they are playing into the hands of the devil who will cause them to suffer great distress. A Christian should have nothing to do with these things. They do not have anything to do with the Spirit of God. Instead they come 'from the Enemy of Christ' (*1 John* 4:3).

We have looked at both Christian and non-Christian religions, at the cults and the occult, at various faiths and philosophies. Is there only one – or are there many – roads to God?

All religions give some insight into the nature of God. Most of them in their search never find God or end up on a 'No Through Road'. Jesus claims to be the direct line to God. 'I am the way, the truth and the life; no-one goes to the Father except by me' (*John* 14:6). This is because Jesus' knowledge of both God and man is unique.

THE CHRISTIAN REVELATION OF GOD

Some religions, eg Buddhism, say that God is unknowable. Others, eg Hinduism, search for God but cannot find him. In *John* 1:18 we read that 'no one has ever seen God. The only Son, who is the same as God and is at the Father's side, he has made him known.'

Christians claim that Jesus is the full and final revelation of God. Some of the sects teach that they have a knowledge of God that goes beyond this. Both Joseph Smith (the Mormon Church) and Sun Myung Moon (the Unification Church) claimed that they had received further revelations from God and the churches they founded are based on this new light that had come to them. The gospels teach that Jesus is the one and only answer to man's salvation. 'God loved the world so much that he gave his only Son, so that everyone who believes in him should not die but have eternal life' (*John* 3:16).

THE CHRISTIAN REVELATION OF MAN

Central to many religions and most philosophies, eg humanism, is the fact that man is basically good and by his own efforts can become a better person. Experience proves to us that we are none of us naturally good. We are 'under the power of sin... there is no one who is righteous' (*Romans* 3:9, 10). Christianity teaches that man has to get rid of his sin before he can begin to live the kind of life that God wants him to live... and this he can only do through Christ.

THE SACRAMENTS

When Jesus founded the Church he provided it with sacraments. A sacrament is a religious rite in which a material object, usually of small value, becomes the outward sign of some spiritual truth which is of great value.

A ROYAL STORY

It is told that one day on her way to Balmoral Queen Victoria called at a cottage and asked for a drink of water. The owner did not recognise her and gave her a drink out of an old cracked cup. When later a neighbour told her who her visitor had been, she said that she would never again touch that cup unless to remind her of her Queen who had once drunk from it.

Jesus, the King of Kings, has given us something else to remind us of him. He has given us water, bread and wine. For Christians these simple things have come to have sacred meaning. In the context of a baptism or a communion service they have a sacramental value because they speak of the love of Jesus.

How often material objects can say so much more than mere words. The man who gives the girl he loves an engagement ring is saying so much more than just 'I love you!' So in the sacraments Jesus is saying in a much more meaningful way to each one of us, 'I love you!'

> 'We get no other thing, nor no new thing, in the
> Sacrament but the same thing which we get in the
> Word – yet we get that same thing better.'
> ROBERT BRUCE, 16th century minister

SACRAMENTUM

This is the Latin word for the oath which a soldier took when he pledged his loyalty to the Roman Emperor. When we receive the sacraments of the Church we are showing our allegiance to Jesus who is our Lord and King.

Some Christian groups, eg the Quakers (Society of Friends) and the Salvation Army have no sacraments. Roman Catholic and Orthodox churches have seven sacraments, ie baptism, confirmation, communion, ordination, marriage, penance and extreme unction.

Other churches single out baptism and communion as the only sacraments which Jesus personally instituted.

'Go to all peoples everywhere and make them my disciples; baptise them ...' *Matthew* 28:19

'This is my body, which is for you. Do this in remembrance of me.' *1 Corinthians* 11:24

BAPTISM

This has always been the sacrament of initiation or introduction into the Christian Church. Practices vary. Some churches give baptism only to believers; others give it to infants on the strength of their parents' faith or that of someone prepared to sponsor them. Baptism may be administered either by sprinkling or pouring water on the forehead, or by immersing in water.

COMMUNION

Baptism can only be given once. Communion will be given many times. It is a constant reminder of Christ's love for those who have been baptised. Bread and wine are used, symbolic of Christ's body and blood. Those who receive communion may do so individually at the hands of the minister or priest, or they may pass the elements from hand to hand among their fellow communicants.

The sacrament goes by different names in different churches.

THE LORD'S SUPPER	*1 Corinthians* 11:20
THE LORD'S TABLE	*1 Corinthians* 10:21
COMMUNION or **FELLOWSHIP**	*1 Corinthians* 10:16
THANKSGIVING or **EUCHARIST**	*1 Corinthians* 11:25
BREAKING OF BREAD	*Acts* 2:42, *RSV*

In Roman Catholic churches it is called the MASS meaning 'Festival' or 'Celebration'. It comes from the Latin *'Ite, missa est ecclesia'* meaning 'Go, the congregation is dismissed.'

WHAT BAPTISM MEANT IN BIBLICAL TIMES

BAPTISM has to do with making a person 'clean' and should not be confused with **CHRISTENING** which has to do with giving a person a Christian name.

Baptism in Jewish times

Jews regarded themselves as already 'clean' and therefore not in need of baptism. They were only clean, however, in a ceremonial sense, eg as Jews they were not debarred from entering a synagogue. Gentiles (non-Jews) did not enjoy this freedom. They had first to be made clean. This meant they required to be circumcised (a minor operation performed on all Jewish male children), and then to baptise themselves.

Baptism–and John the Baptist

John the Baptist spoke about the need for everyone, Jew and Gentile alike, to be baptised. He demanded not ceremonial, but moral, cleansing. 'Turn away from your sins and be baptised', he said, 'and God will forgive your sins' (*Luke* 3:3).

Baptism – and Jesus Christ

Jesus baptised (*John* 3:22) and gave instructions to his disciples to baptise (*Matthew* 28:19). First, however, he asked to be baptised himself by John the Baptist (*Matthew* 3:13–17). Though he was without sin, he wanted to identify himself completely with those who had sinned and who needed to be baptised.

Baptism in Jesus' name gave cleansing from sin but also the gift of the Holy Spirit. Peter said to his converts, 'Each of you must turn away from his sins and be baptised in the name of Jesus Christ, so that your sins will be forgiven you; and you will receive God's gift, the Holy Spirit' (*Acts* 2:38).

Those who were baptised could identify themselves with Jesus' death and resurrection. A person to be baptised was immersed in water and then came up out of the water to begin a new life in Christ. It was like being buried, becoming dead to sin and rising again to a new life. Paul says, 'By our baptism we were buried with him and shared his death, in order that, just as Christ was raised from death by the glorious power of the Father, so also we might live a new life' (*Romans* 6:4).

WHAT BAPTISM MEANS IN MODERN TIMES

The meaning of baptism is the same at whatever age or stage it takes place. When someone who has a Christian faith is baptised, he or she will understand what it means at the time. In the case of an infant there can be no understanding at the time but it is a promise made to the child. When he or she grows up to have a personal faith, then baptism will come to have meaning for that person. Here are three things which baptism means today.

CLEANSING FROM SIN

Paul says, 'Everyone has sinned and is far away from God's saving presence' (*Romans* 3:23). An infant has no awareness of sin but he or she has nevertheless inherited the sin of Adam (see p 21). As Christians we believe that on the cross Jesus takes our sin upon himself and makes us clean. The pouring or sprinkling of water in baptism is a symbol of that cleansing.

UNION WITH CHRIST

In baptism we are united with Christ and become identified with him in every way. 'When we were baptised into union with Christ Jesus, we were baptised into union with his death' (*Romans* 6:3). We are also, however, united with him in his resurrection. We share his risen life. The union, however, may not be immediately evident. It has taken place but like any union – a union between two churches, for example – it may be some time before it really comes to mean anything.

Paul describes what has happened in terms of grafting. 'A wild olive', he says, 'can be grafted against all nature into a cultivated olive' (*Romans* 11:24). It may take many months before the grafted branch bears good fruit but the union has been made. Similarly in baptism we are grafted into Christ and should 'grow up in every way to Christ' (*Ephesians* 4:15).

LIVING IN THE SPIRIT

In baptism we are given the Holy Spirit to help us live 'in fellowship with God through Christ Jesus' (*Romans* 6:11). We must believe that God's Spirit is with us. 'If Christ lives in you, the Spirit is life for you because you have been put right with God' (*Romans* 8:10).

INFANT BAPTISM

Infant baptism – in the New Testament

While there is no precise instruction in the New Testament about baptising infants, it was the practice in the Church from a very early date. The first followers of Jesus would be adults and would, therefore, be baptised as believers. By the next generation the whole situation had changed. In *Acts* 16 we read about both a household and a family which received baptism, and this must almost certainly have included children.

Baptism is a sacrament of the New Covenant. Under the Old Covenant children were made holy, ie acceptable to God, because they belonged to the community of God's people. The mark of this was the circumcision of baby boys. Under the New Covenant children are brought into the family of Christ and into the fellowship of his Church on the strength of their parent's faith – or that of someone prepared to act for the parents. The mark of this is the baptism of infants. This is the way in which the New Covenant is sealed. As Peter said, it is a promise made by God 'to you and to your children' (*Acts* 2:39).

Infant baptism – objections to the practice

(a) Some would argue that baptism should only be given to believers. No one would deny the right of a person who has not been baptised as an infant to be baptised on making his or her own confession of faith. Baptism, however, is also a sign of God's acceptance of us before we have any personal faith or understanding of what that means. In baptism God declares his love for all children before they can even speak his name.

(b) Some would argue that baptism does no good to the infant concerned. Baptism, however, is not like a vaccination which is given as a safeguard against future sinning. It is rather God's chosen way to introduce us to the life of faith. A person baptised in infancy is immediately brought within the family of the Church and there, under the Christian influence of parents and congregation, the seeds of faith are implanted and spiritual growth is encouraged.

THE ORIGIN OF THE LAST SUPPER

> The day came during the Festival of Unleavened Bread when the lambs for the Passover meal were to be killed. Jesus sent off Peter and John with these instructions, 'Go and get the Passover meal ready for us to eat.'
>
> *Luke* 22:7

The festival was in April and lasted for a week. On the first night the Passover was celebrated. It commemorated God's deliverance of the Israelites from slavery in Egypt (see *Exodus* 12). They had been ordered by Moses to smear the lintel and the sideposts of their doors with the blood of a lamb. That night death struck every Egyptian home and took as its victim the first-born in each family. The homes of the Israelites, however, were spared. Death 'passed over' the houses of God's people. Before leaving Egypt they prepared a hurried meal which they called the Passover. It included lamb, bitter herbs, such as parsley, to remind them of bitter times spent under the Egyptians, and unleavened bread – because there was no time to put in the leaven or the yeast before the bread was baked.

THE PASSOVER

The Passover is still celebrated in many Jewish homes. Before it there is a ceremonial search by candlelight to rid the house of leaven (see *Exodus* 12:15). The meal is a happy family occasion and during it the story of the first Passover is told all over again.

Jesus celebrated the Passover with his disciples in a house in Jerusalem. He had arranged for a man who was carrying a water-jug (an uncommon sight) to lead Peter and John to the house. There in an upstairs room they prepared the meal and later Jesus and the other disciples sat down to celebrate the feast. During it Jesus gave it a new meaning.

> He took a piece of bread, gave thanks to God, broke it, and gave it to them saying, 'This is my body, which is given for you. Do this in memory of me.' In the same way he gave the cup after the supper saying, 'This cup is God's new covenant sealed with my blood, which is poured out for you.'
>
> *1 Corinthians* 11:23–25

From that day this meal reminded his followers of the new Passover, of how God through Jesus had delivered them from sin.

THE LORD'S SUPPER—THE LOVE FEAST

'Day after day they met as a group in the Temple, and they had their meals together in their homes, eating with glad and humble hearts, praising God, and enjoying the good-will of all the people.'

Acts 2:46–47

There is little doubt that the Lord's Supper as it was celebrated by the first Christians was a family meal or a meal with friends in a private house. They welcomed this because the poorer among them often got little enough to eat. Its chief value, however, was the fellowship it provided for the Christian community. For that reason it came to be known as the *Agape* or Love Feast.

The Lord's Supper today takes a very different form from what it did then. All but the wine and the bread have been removed from the meal and these only have symbolic meaning. Despite this we should never celebrate the Lord's Supper without at the same time being aware of the fellowship that we share with other Christians. This is not always easy in the traditionally large service which is characteristic of the Scottish communion. Sometimes it is more meaningful to have only a small number gathering for the sacrament or to link it with some special event in the Church's life, eg a conference or a retreat.

We should always remember that the Lord's Supper is never a private meal. Jesus is the host and we are the guests. It is he who invites us to his table and the invitation is to all those who love him. That is why we must never exclude anyone from sharing in this sacrament.

The only time when a person is not welcome is when he or she has fallen out with someone. Any dispute or quarrel must first be put right. 'Everyone should examine himself first, and then eat the bread and drink the cup' (*1 Corinthians* 11:28). The Lord's Supper is a love feast and those who share in it must be at one with their neighbour and with Christ.

THE SACRAMENT OF THE LORD'S SUPPER

The Lord's Supper — a commemorative meal

Jesus said, 'Do this in memory of me' *1 Corinthians* 11:24.

In this sacrament we remember that Jesus gave his life for us. 'The greatest love a person can have for his friends is to give his life for them' (*John* 15:13). The bread and wine are symbols of the sacrifice he made, of his body and blood.

As we celebrate the sacrament we do not just remember that Jesus died. We remember also that he rose again and that he is still with us. Jesus who 'died for our sins...was raised to life three days later' (*1 Corinthians* 15:3, 4). At the Lord's Supper we are commemorating both his death and his resurrection, his earthly life and his life with us now.

A LEGEND ABOUT ZACCHAEUS

It is told that sometimes Zacchaeus would vanish and no-one would know where he had gone. One day a friend followed him and saw him walk along a certain road. At a particular tree he stopped. His friend went up to him and asked him, 'Why do you come and stand beside this tree?' 'It was from this tree', said Zacchaeus, 'that I first saw my Lord, and when I get all hot and bothered or tempted to go back to my old way of life, I come out here and stand beside this tree, and I remember him, and I'm alright again.'

The Lord's Supper — a communion meal

Jesus said, 'Whoever eats my flesh and drinks my blood lives in me, and I live in him.'

John 6:56

The Roman Catholic teaching is that in the sacrament the bread and wine become for the believer the body and blood of Christ but retain the appearance of bread and wine. Protestants would hold the view that when Jesus instituted this sacrament, he was holding a piece of bread in his hand and when he said, 'This is my body', the disciples would interpret this as meaning 'This represents my body'. The bread and the wine are but symbols of Christ's body and blood but when the believer eats and drinks of them, he is in a very real sense taking Jesus into his own heart and life, making him a part of himself. He knows then that Christ lives in him.

The Lord's Supper – a thanksgiving meal

'He took a cup, gave thanks to God, and handed it to them.'

Mark 14:23

Some churches call this sacrament 'the eucharist'. This comes from the Greek word for 'he gave thanks'. As Jesus was full of gratitude for all that God had done for him, so we can be grateful for all that God has done for us through him. We give thanks for all the gifts of God, not least for the gift of our lives and the gift of Jesus. So often there is no sense of real thanksgiving in a communion service. It should be a time for celebration and rejoicing.

'This is the hour of banquet and of song'

In an ancient communion thanksgiving prayer we are reminded that all around us there are thousands of people in heaven and on earth who are all praising God. This is how it begins:

IT IS VERY MEET, RIGHT, AND OUR BOUNDEN DUTY THAT WE SHOULD AT ALL TIMES, AND IN ALL PLACES, GIVE THANKS UNTO THEE, O LORD, HOLY FATHER, ALMIGHTY, EVERLASTING GOD.
THEREFORE WITH ANGELS AND ARCHANGELS, AND WITH ALL THE COMPANY OF HEAVEN, WE LAUD AND MAGNIFY THY GLORIOUS NAME, EVERMORE PRAISING THEE AND SAYING, HOLY, HOLY, HOLY, LORD GOD OF HOSTS, HEAVEN AND EARTH ARE FULL OF THY GLORY.

The Lord's Supper – a proclamation meal

'Every time you eat this bread and drink from this cup you proclaim the Lord's death until he come.'

1 Corinthians 11:26

This sacrament is a visual presentation of Jesus' death. On Palm Sunday he proclaimed that he was King of peace by riding into Jerusalem on the back of a donkey (the animal of peace). So here in the breaking of bread Christians proclaim that Jesus died for their sins but it is in the expectation that one day he will return in glory. This sacrament looks back to what Jesus did on the cross but it looks forward always to his coming again. It is this expectation which gives freshness to the sacrament even when its meaning becomes dulled by frequent celebration.

THE SCOTTISH COMMUNION

The symbols of communion

THE CROSS
THE CUP
THE LOAF

In Scotland after the Reformation it became the practice to celebrate communion once every three months. This infrequency after the former weekly celebration led to what was called 'The Communion Season'. The main celebration was preceded by preparatory services and ended with 'The Thanksgiving'. Different ministers used to take part in these services.

Preparation for communion was strict and systematic. Every intending communicant was catechised, ie examined on the Shorter Catechism, the Lord's Prayer, the Creed and the Commandments. This was the responsibility of the minister and the Kirk Session. If they were satisfied as to the communicant's knowledge and character, they would issue a communion token, a metal or leather disc bearing the name of the particular church.

Today the sacrament is often held more frequently but it is still a solemn occasion in the life of the Church. The usual practice today is for the elder to give a communion card to those members in his district who are 'in full communion' though this is not to exclude others from sharing in the sacrament. The card is more a reminder and invitation than a ticket of admission.

The Church of Scotland has an open communion, ie all who belong to any branch of the Christian Church are invited to partake. The table is traditionally covered with 'a fine white linen cloth' and sometimes the pews are similarly covered. The minister and elders sit round the table on which the communion elements have been laid before the service. In some churches they are brought in during the singing prior to the sacrament.

The minister officiates by using the words spoken by Jesus at the Last Supper. He and the elders then partake of the bread and the wine. After this these elements are taken round the congregation who remain in their seats and they are passed from one to the other by hand. While a single cup will be used at the table, individual cups are often used to pass round the pews.

The Bible is not a single book. It contains sixty-six separate books. In a library they would appear under different headings. The Greek word *biblia* means 'the little books'. They could be grouped into two sections: the Old Testament (BC, or Before Christ) and the New Testament (AD, or *Anno Domini*, in the Year of our Lord).

OLD TESTAMENT – originally in Hebrew. Thirty-nine books.

Law books	GENESIS, EXODUS, LEVITICUS, NUMBERS and DEUTERONOMY. Known as the Law; in Hebrew, *Torah*; in Greek, *Pentateuch* which means 'five books'. Contain history and laws of the Israelite people.
History books	JOSHUA to ESTHER. Historical record covering period of the Judges and the Kings of Israel and Judah.
Poetry books	PSALMS, PROVERBS, SONG OF SOLOMON and ECCLESIASTES. JOB is Hebrew philosophy.
Prophetic books	ISAIAH to EZEKIEL are the major prophets. HOSEA to MALACHI are the minor prophets. DANIEL, a book about the future, stands on its own.

NEW TESTAMENT – originally in Greek. Twenty-seven books.

The Gospels	MATTHEW, MARK, LUKE, JOHN. Gospel means good news, glad tidings, or in the Chinese idiom, happy sound. Tell the story of Jesus' birth, life, death and resurrection.
The Acts	ACTS OF THE APOSTLES told by Luke.
The Letters	ROMANS to JUDE. Letters, sometimes known as epistles, written by Paul and others to different churches and individuals.
The Revelation	REVELATION to JOHN, an exiled Christian. Told in symbolic language to encourage other Christians at a time when they were being persecuted.

(.

The third vow (first part)

DO YOU PROMISE TO BE FAITHFUL IN READING THE BIBLE?

The Bible is probably the best-known–and yet at the same time the least-known–of all the books in the world. It has been written, of course, by many people. It contains a great variety of different kinds of literature: story, history, poetry, prose, prophecy, parables, letters, etc. Through them all runs a single thread God revealing his purpose for mankind. Each author writes from his own point of view and period in time but all point, directly or otherwise, to Jesus Christ.

HOW SHOULD WE BEGIN TO READ THE BIBLE?

1. Get a translation that you can understand. Some like the traditional versions but more and more prefer a modern translation. A list of Bibles currently available is printed on p 88. For new readers we would recommend the Bible that has been used in this guide–the GOOD NEWS BIBLE.

2. There is no great virtue in reading the Bible through from *Genesis* to *Revelation*. It is better to start with one of the records of the life and teaching of Jesus. Mark's gospel is the shortest and also the first to be written. It is a good one to start with. Read it slowly and with imagination. If you have time, read the whole sixteen chapters at a stretch. Let the characters in it come to life and discover that Jesus is not just a name in print, but a living person. As the writer John Ruskin once said, 'Be present, as if in the body, at each recorded event in the life of the Redeemer.' From there you can go on to read the other gospels, or *The Acts,* or one of the letters of Paul, or some Old Testament books.

3. The Bible is full of difficult passages but don't be put off by that. There are many commentaries or explanatory notes to show what it means. Perhaps the most useful thing you can get is a Bible reading guide. This gives a suggested passage to be read each day and adds a comment or explanation, and sometimes a prayer. A list of suitable reading guides is printed on p 88.

How the Bible came to be written

The Bible used by Jesus was our Old Testament. The books in it formed the Jewish scriptures and were known as 'the law and the prophets'. The Christian Church continued to use the Old Testament but saw the need for other books to describe the new faith. Some of Paul's letters and later the gospels came to be regarded as authoritative – the writers had all either known Jesus personally or had known someone who knew him. Gradually these books were gathered together and became the canon (ie the standard of faith) of the New Testament. Other books regarded by the Protestant churches as having less authority have been included in some Bibles, eg those used by the Roman Catholic Church. These books form the Apocrypha, ie books which are 'hidden' or have unknown authorship.

How the Bible can be the Word of God

In church the minister may introduce the scripture reading by saying, 'Let us hear the Word of God.' God 'speaks' to us as we read the Bible and 'listen for his voice'. It is the Holy Spirit using the words of the Bible to say something to us.

We must not think that every word of the Bible has been directly inspired by God. This is a popularly held belief. The words of our Bible are a translation of the original Hebrew and Greek text. Translations vary tremendously and are to help us to understand what the Bible is actually saying. Notes or a commentary will help us to interpret the Bible correctly.

The Word of God became a living person in Jesus Christ. He is the embodiment or incarnation of God's Word. 'In the past, God spoke to our ancestors many times and in many ways through the prophets but in these last days he has spoken to us through his Son' (*Hebrews* 1:1–2). 'The Word became a human being' (*John* 1:14).

How the Bible can be relied on

Some people will not recognise the authority of the Bible because it appears to contain errors and contradictions. If there are inconsistencies, these will be explained by resorting to a commentary and discovering what lies behind them. The main purpose of the Bible – to record the loving purpose of God in Jesus Christ – is not affected by these difficulties.

THE BIBLE—A SPAN OF HISTORY

GENESIS
2800 BC

Abraham belonged to a Bedouin tribe. Looking for pasture for his flocks he and his family left Ur in Babylonia and travelled along the Euphrates River to Haran, and then to Canaan where they eventually settled. Abraham had a son, Isaac, and a grandson, Jacob (also called Israel). Israel had twelve sons and their families are often known as the Twelve Tribes of Israel. One of the sons, Joseph, was sold by his brothers who were jealous of him to some travellers and thus he came to be in Egypt. There he won the approval of the King of Egypt (known as Pharaoh) and was put in charge of food supplies during a time of world famine. His whole family came to Egypt looking for corn and after being reunited with Joseph they settled there.

EXODUS
1300 BC

JOSHUA

1225 BC

A pharaoh known as Rameses II turned the Israelite settlers into slaves. Moses went to Egypt to lead them out of that land and bring them back to Canaan, the Promised Land. The journey took forty years. Near the end of it Moses died and Joshua took over the leadership. When they settled again in Canaan they were first ruled over by JUDGES and then later became a nation under King David. At first they prospered. Then they adopted the practices of the heathen tribes on their borders and this was the beginning of their downfall.

KINGS
1000 BC

CHRONICLES
586 BC

445 BC

Solomon became king in place of his father, David. After his reign the nation split into a northern kingdom, Israel (capital, Samaria) and a southern kingdom, Judah (capital, Jerusalem). Eventually both kingdoms collapsed and the Israelites were exiled to Babylon. Jerusalem was destroyed but later the walls were rebuilt under the leadership of NEHEMIAH, and the people returned.

GOSPELS
70 AD

ACTS

From this time the Israelites (or Jews, as they were now called) were never independent. In Jesus' day they were subject to Rome. Jerusalem was again destroyed but Christian missionaries had now become active all over the Mediterranean. Churches were founded in many places, including Rome, the capital of the Empire.

HOW THE BIBLE CAME TO BE WRITTEN

The earliest stories of the Bible were passed down by word of mouth. When trading began between nations, so there arose a need for writing. At first it was in the form of pictures, then of letters.

The earliest writing was done on clay tablets or pieces of pottery. Then papyrus reeds were gathered from the river banks. Thin strips of their pith were laid criss-cross on each other to produce a kind of 'paper' (from the word papyrus). The scriptures were written column by column on lengths of tanned skin (scrolls) which were rolled up and kept in a synagogue. In 1947 a Bedouin shepherd boy came across a collection of scrolls in some stone jars in a cave near the Dead Sea. They were found to contain some of the earliest original text of the Bible and are known as the Dead Sea Scrolls.

The Old Testament scriptures were written in Hebrew but the spoken language was Aramaic. There are examples of Aramaic in *Mark* 5:41 and *Matthew* 27:46. The New Testament was written in Greek. Greek, like English, is read from left to right but Hebrew is read from right to left. Also, the Hebrew Bible begins at what we would call the end. There are often no spaces between Hebrew words and the vowels are the little dots above and below the line. Here are the first words of the *Book of Genesis* – IN THE BEGINNING – written first in Hebrew, then in Greek.

בְּרֵאשִׁית   'Εν ἀρχῇ

The New Testament was not written till long after Jesus' day. At the time when he died, people thought that he was going to come back – as he said he would one day – in their own lifetime. When it became apparent that this was not going to happen, they began to write down their memories of his life, his death and his resurrection. The earliest book we have is Paul's *Letter to the Thessalonians* – AD 50 – and the first gospel, that of Mark, followed ten years later in AD 60.

270 BC	Publication of the SEPTUAGINT, a Greek translation of the Old Testament. The name meant 'seventy' and referred to the number of scholars involved in the work.
385 AD	St Jerome translated the whole Bible into Latin. This version was known as the VULGATE from the Latin *vulgare* meaning 'to make public'. It was the first authorised version to be used by the Roman Catholic Church.
1342 AD	Only the priests could understand Latin. John Wycliffe realised that ordinary people could not read the Bible for themselves. 'To be ignorant of the Scriptures', he said, 'is to be ignorant of Christ.' He then translated Jerome's Latin Bible into English.
	At first the Bible had to be written out in longhand. Monks spent many hours copying the scriptures and produced very beautiful Bibles. With the invention of
1450 AD	printing it became possible to make Bibles more widely available. The first printer of the English Bible was Miles Coverdale. He was followed by William Tyndale who had to do much of his work on the continent because of opposition from the church in England. Tyndale was eventually burnt at the stake.
1604 AD	King James VI of Scotland and I of England ordered a new official translation of the Bible. This became the
1611 AD	AUTHORISED VERSION, sometimes known as the King James Version.
	In our own time a variety of modern versions of the Bible has been published. One that received the official blessing
1970 AD	of all the main churches was the NEW ENGLISH BIBLE.

Today the Bible has found its way into almost every country in the world. This has been largely due to the work of the Bible Societies which translate, print and distribute Bibles in many lands. Their aim is to give everyone a Bible in that person's own native language and at a price that he or she can afford to pay. The letters in the sign above are those of the National Bible Society of Scotland.

The third vow (second part)

DO YOU PROMISE TO BE FAITHFUL IN PRAYER?

With the folding of hands
There's a spreading of wings,
And the soul's lifted up
With invisible hands,
And ineffable peace.

Evelyn Underhill

PRAYERS FOR A BUSY PERSON

At the beginning of each day
This day belongs to the Lord. Let me enjoy it to the full and give him all the praise.

On beginning a meal
For life and love and home and food, we thank you, heavenly Father.

On opening the Bible
As I read your Word, let it speak to me of your love.

In time of temptation
Let me never forget, Lord, that you see our thoughts as well as our deeds. Give me help to overcome my temptation.

A family prayer
Father of us all, I remember before you my family and your family. Watch over them and keep them safe.

On going to bed
As I sleep, let me remember that you stay awake. Look after my cares and give me a good night's rest.

ON HOW TO PRAY

1. You can pray kneeling, standing, sitting, lying. Use the position that helps you to concentrate on what you are doing.

2. 'Be aware of the Lord's presence' (Psalm 16:8). 'He is near to those who call to him, who call to him with sincerity' (Psalm 145:18). Believe that God is close beside you and talk to him as a friend.

3. You can picture God from the pictures given of him in the Bible. The Psalms are particularly helpful here. Jesus described him as 'our Father in heaven'.

4. Prayer doesn't require special language. God understands you whatever words you use. Address him as 'Thou', 'Thee' or 'You', whichever you find most meaningful.

5. Jesus said, 'When you pray, do not use a lot of meaningless words, as the pagans do, who think that God will hear them because their prayers are long' (*Matthew* 6:7). A long, wordy prayer is no more effective than a short one.

6. Do not show off in prayer. Jesus said, 'The hypocrites love to stand and pray in the houses of worship and on street corners, so that everyone will see them ... When you pray, go to your room, close the door and pray to your Father, who is unseen' *(Matthew* 5:6). Edward Wilson who sailed with Captain Scott on his expedition to the South Pole used the crow's nest of the ship as what he called 'my private chapel'. If you don't have a separate room in which to pray, find a compartment of your mind where you can be alone with God.

7. Be honest in your prayers. 'No one makes a fool of God' (*Galatians* 6:7). Martin Luther once said, 'Don't lie to God!' God knows what you are thinking even though you say something quite different to him. So be straight with him.

THE LORD'S PRAYER

Jesus gave his disciples this prayer to be a pattern for all prayer. There are two traditional versions: *Matthew* 6:9–15 in the *Authorised Version* and the *English Prayer Book* version which uses 'trespasses' instead of 'debts'. The doxology – 'For Thine is the Kingdom, the Power and the Glory' – is not found in the scripture version.

Our Father which art in heaven, hallowed be thy name

God is like a perfect human father (see *Matthew* 7:11). This sets a right relationship between God and ourselves. We are to think of God as 'our Father' and this gives us a right relationship with each other. 'Hallowed' means 'to be treated as holy'.

Thy kingdom come, thy will be done in earth, as it is in heaven

The kingdom of God is a society on earth in which God's will is as perfectly done as it is in heaven. In praying for his kingdom to come everywhere, we should first pray for it to come in our own lives. As an old Negro prayer has it, 'Bring in the Kingdom, Lord, and begin it with me.'

Give us this day our daily bread

We are to live by the day and to give no anxious thought to tomorrow (*Matthew* 6:25–34). The future is in God's hands. What we must ask for is bread – not cake; for the necessities and not for the luxuries.

Forgive us our debts as we forgive our debtors

'Give' is followed by 'forgive'. God will only forgive us if we are forgiving towards others (read the story in *Matthew* 18:23–25). 'Debt' suggests that we owe God something. 'Trespasses' implies that we have crossed some forbidden line. Both words mean 'sin'.

And lead us not into temptation, but deliver us from evil

The biblical word 'tempt' has the idea of testing in it. The *NEB* version reads, 'Do not bring us to the test'. Our prayer is that God may protect us from temptation and help us to resist all evil, or the evil one.

DIFFERENT KINDS OF PRAYER

Both in public and in private prayer there should be some order in the things we pray about. The order need not always be the same but here are some suggestions which may be helpful.

ADORATION
Looking at God's greatness

'The Lord is great and is to be highly praised' (Psalm 143:3). Sir Thomas Browne once said, 'Think magnificently about God.' We can have homely thoughts about God as 'our Father' but we should never forget that he is also great beyond our understanding or imagining.

CONFESSION
Admitting faults, failings and shortcomings

'Examine me, O God, and know my mind; test me, and discover my thoughts' (Psalm 139:32). Martin Luther once said that prayer time is God's punishment time. It is certainly a time for self-examination and confession before God.

Confession of sin must be followed by absolution. 'If we confess our sins to God, he will forgive us our sins and purify us from all our wrongdoing' (*1 John* 1:9). We must believe that God absolves or acquits us of every sin that we confess before him.

SUPPLICATION
Asking for help, strength and guidance

If we are going to live in the way that God wants us to live, we must recognise that we cannot do this without his help.

Supplication may take the form of a prayer for guidance when we cannot see clearly the direction we ought to be travelling or the decision we ought to be taking. Pray about it and then act as though God is guiding you to do the right thing.

Supplication may also take the form of a prayer for grace, ie freely given help. God is more willing to give us help than we are to ask for it. Pray for grace to meet any particular situation and then believe that God will give you the strength and help you need.

THANKSGIVING
Being grateful

This must be the dominant note in all Christian prayer. Many people will want to start their prayers by giving thanks, telling God how grateful they are for all he has given them. He is a God who 'has done wonderful things' (*Psalm* 98:1).

Give thanks to God for life itself, for health and happiness, for human skills and abilities, for the world in which we live with all it has to offer, for the sounds and sights of nature, for music and art, for books and pictures, for food and clothes, for heat and light, for our homes, for family life, for the circle of our friends; for everything that makes life richer and fuller and better.

Above all, remember with thanksgiving that 'God, who generously gives us everything for our enjoyment' (*1 Timothy* 6:17), has also given us his most precious possession, his Son Jesus. 'He gave us his Son – will he not also freely give us all things?' (*Romans* 8:32). Because of this we can thank God for everything, the bad things as well as the good things, for they all have a place in his purpose of love. When depressed or up against it, we should remember the words of an old Scottish saint called Halyburton, 'I can pull myself back into the sunshine through the duty of thankfulness.'

INTERCESSION
Praying for others

Paul once said, 'I urge that petitions, prayers, requests, and thanksgivings be offered to God for all people' (*1 Timothy* 2:1). Intercession, praying for others, prevents us from thinking only of our own needs. In practice we should pray first for our immediate family and friends and their needs, and then for our local community, our country, the whole world and that Christ's kingdom be established everywhere. Only God knows all the needs of the world; let us pray for those known to us, and those needs known to God alone.

67

UNDERSTANDING THE NATURE OF PRAYER

Here are some suggestions on how we ought to approach prayer.

Be specific

Don't be vague in the things you pray about. Be precise and definite. God is interested in detail. 'Even the hairs of your head have all been counted' (*Matthew* 10:30). If a thing is important to you, it is also important to God. Nothing is too trivial to be brought before him in prayer.

Be expectant

Sometimes we pray for something to happen and nothing does happen. We should then ask ourselves whether we really expected something to happen. People pray for miracles but often they don't really expect the miracle to happen. God is a great God and we should never underestimate his power. When a man once asked Jesus if he would heal his son, Jesus replied, 'Everything is possible for the person who has faith' (*Mark* 9:23 – see reference to this story on p 5). We must believe that God can do the impossible.

Be persevering

If we do not get an answer to our prayers, we should go on asking. Jesus told a story about a man who had to go on knocking at his friend's door before he could persuade him to open up and give him some bread (see *Luke* 11:5–13). When Jesus said, 'Knock, and the door will be opened to you' (*Matthew* 7:7), he didn't say how long we must keep knocking. God is always willing to give us what is good for us but he must know first that we really want it. Persistent knocking is sometimes a measure of how anxious we are to get what we ask for.

Be content

If you pray earnestly for something and you don't get what you pray for, accept that it is not for you. Paul had a painful physical ailment. Some have suggested that he suffered from severe headaches. 'Three times', he tells us, 'I prayed to the Lord about this and asked him to take it away.' He didn't. Instead he said, 'My grace is all you need' (*2 Corinthians* 12:8, 9). If God doesn't give us exactly what we ask for, he will give us help – grace – to accept the situation as it is.

GIVING FOR THE WORK OF THE CHURCH

The fourth vow

**DO YOU PROMISE TO GIVE
A FITTING PROPORTION
OF YOUR TIME, TALENTS AND MONEY
FOR THE CHURCH'S WORK
IN THE WORLD?**

All thinking and teaching about Christian giving begins with God. God has given us everything we have, our lives included. Everything we give to God, therefore, has already been given to us by God. If we had anything of our own, we would be able to take it with us when we die. Job discovered a long time ago that this wasn't the case.

> 'I was born with nothing, and I will die with nothing.
> The Lord gave, and now he has taken away.'
>
> *Job* 1:21

The Christian may feel he owns the world but the world is not his – it belongs to God.

> 'Everything belongs to you ... this world, life and death, the present and the future – all these are yours, and you belong to Christ, and Christ belongs to God.'
>
> *1 Corinthians* 3:22, 23

A STORY

A boy was given a present of a model yacht. He sailed it one day in the sea and lost it. Some time later he saw his boat for sale in a shop window. Somebody had found it and sold it to the shopkeeper. The boy went in and claimed that it was his boat. The shopkeeper said that the only way he could get it back would be to buy it. The boy paid the money, picked up his boat and said, 'You were mine, but now you are doubly mine. I lost you and I have paid to get you back.'

We belong to God because he made us. Because of our sin he has lost us. Now he has bought us back, making Jesus the payment for our sin. Paul writes, 'You do not belong to yourselves but to God; he bought you for a price' (*1 Corinthians* 6:20).

THE QUESTION OF CHRISTIAN GIVING

To help people understand his teaching about God and the kingdom, Jesus used to tell stories or parables. In *Matthew* 21:33–44 he tells a parable which makes us think of how much – or how little – we give to God.

Background to the story

It was not unusual for a landowner to let out his ground to tenants and then to go and live elsewhere. The owner of this vineyard did just that. First, however, he equipped it with everything necessary to ensure a good harvest. He protected it with a fence, dug a hole for a winepress, and built a watchtower to guard it against thieves. In due course he sent messengers to collect the rent from the tenants. The tenants, rather than pay the rent, got rid of the messengers. He sent other messengers and the same thing happened. In the end he sent his own son. 'Surely they will respect my son', he said – but they treated him worse than the others. He was thrown out of the vineyard and put to death. The story ends by saying that the landowner paid off these tenants and found other tenants who would have a proper regard for himself and his property.

...and some thoughts for ourselves

The chief priests and the Pharisees who heard the story knew that Jesus was speaking about their own people. God had given them every privilege. He had made them his chosen race. In return he looked for their loyalty and love and devotion. But how did they react? When he sent his messengers, ie the prophets to remind them of their responsibilities, they stoned them to death. When he sent his son Jesus, they crucified him. Everything God had given them they kept and gave him nothing in return. What would God do to them now?

Consider all the things that God has given you, life and the things you possess. What have you given him back of your time, of your talents, of your money? What rent have you paid for the privilege of enjoying so many of his gifts? Is God saying something to you in this parable by way of warning? Is there a lesson to be learnt about Christian giving?

THE USE OF OUR TIME

The clock is a symbol of time, one of God's gifts to us. The Bible says what a man's life-span is. 'Seventy years is all we have ... eighty years, if we are strong' (Psalm 90:10). None of us knows, in fact, how long we will live. The important thing, says Paul, is to 'be careful how you live ... make good use of every opportunity you have' (*Ephesians* 5:15, 16). There are some people who can live as full a life in thirty years as others will live in twice that time.

THERE IS A TIME FOR EVERY MATTER UNDER HEAVEN
Ecclesiastes 3:1, *RSV*

A fact we cannot disregard

Jesus said, 'A day has twelve hours, hasn't it?' (*John* 11:9). The length of daylight may vary in different parts of the world and at different times of the year. Nevertheless, God gives us the day for working and the night for sleeping. Jesus said, 'As long as it is day, we must keep on doing the work of him who sent me; night is coming when no-one can work' (*John* 9:4). By this he meant that we have only got so long to do all the work that God plans for us to do in our lifetime.

... and some questions to think about:

Am I making the best use of my time?

Am I using each day in the way that a Christian should? Do I sometimes fritter my time away or am I always looking at my watch and wondering if I can get everything done?

Do I spend long enough reading my Bible, in prayer, with God? Do I give enough time to be with my family? Do I spend more time on leisure than on work, or do I overwork and never relax?

THE USE OF OUR TALENTS

Jesus tells another parable (*Matthew* 25:14–30) about a man who divided his belongings among his three servants and gave to them respectively five talents, two talents and one talent. The first two invested their talents and doubled the amount. The third buried his talent. When the man returned to ask what they had done with their talents, the two gave back their talents with profit; the other returned the talent as he had been given it. Jesus said that because he had not used his talent, it would be taken away from him. And so with our talents – if we do not use them, we lose them. In the original story the talents were sums of money (in the *NEB* 'bags of gold'). Our talents could well be our aptitudes and abilities, our skills and expertise. We may not have unlimited resources but, the parable suggests, we all have at least one talent.

WHAT CAN YOU DO?

We can all do different things. One person can type; another can cook. A manufacturer can make things; a mechanic can mend things. One man can do a skilled job with his hands; another is able to think things out and make vital decisions. Everyone has something that he or she can do. For some it will be a labouring job; for others it will require specialised knowledge. Whatever talent you have, use it to the full and give the glory to God.

A QUOTE

God does not want extraordinary people who do extraordinary things nearly as much as he wants ordinary people who do ordinary things extraordinarily well.

Money is only a token of the value which we put on things, eg a meal out, a television set, a pair of shoes, a bus journey. Even though we have earned our money, it came originally from God. It is God who provides the raw materials from which man is able to produce the things that we use in life and which can be purchased with money which represents the value we put on them.

Take a loaf of bread, for example. We buy it from the baker's shop or the supermarket but we can also trace it back to its beginnings:

> Back of the loaf is the snowy flour,
> Back of the flour, the mill,
> Back of the mill is the wheat and the shower,
> And the sun, and the Father's will.

Because our money comes originally from God, so we are responsible to him for the use we make of it.

MONEY — TO USE OR TO ABUSE

The Bible does not say that there is anything wrong with money as such but that 'the love of money is the root of all evil' (*1 Timothy* 6:10, *AV*). The desire for money can only make a person discontented, as these stories told by Jesus illustrate.

Luke 12:13–21	A businessman spends his whole life making money and then discovers too late that he can't take it with him when he dies.
Luke 16:19–31	A wealthy man (usually known as Dives) is punished in the afterlife for only looking after himself and giving nothing to a beggar called Lazarus who was desperately poor.
Luke 18:18–25	A rich young man finds that having many possessions doesn't make him happy. He is told that the only answer is to sell everything and give his money to the poor—but this he cannot bring himself to do.

USING OUR TIME, TALENTS AND MONEY IN THE WORK OF THE CHURCH

If our time, talents and money have been given us by God, then we must give at least 'a fitting proportion' of them for the Church's work in the world. Here are some ways in which this can be done.

The Church's work in the congregation

As a member of the Church your first loyalty is to your local congregation. You must give of your time to share in worship and other activities within your church, and you must also give money for its maintenance and its upkeep. You may also be able to use your particular talents to help with the work of the congregation, eg:

> Looking after the fabric and keeping the grounds;
> Doing secretarial work or keeping accounts;
> Teaching in Sunday school, Bible class, etc;
> Helping with youth or other organisations;
> Visiting people in their homes or in hospital;
> Giving, arranging or distributing flowers;
> Preparing, producing and delivering magazines and leaflets;
> Singing in the choir or helping to lead the worship, etc etc.

The Church's work in the community

If your church is doing its job properly, it will be at the centre of the community in which it is situated. As a member of it you may be able to help with voluntary organisations or in local government. You will also have a missionary responsibility within the community and must help to bring those who live near you into the life and fellowship of your congregation.

The Church's work in the world

The work of the Church is worldwide and as a member of a local congregation you must support this work by finding out about it, by praying about it, and by giving money to help it. You may be able to serve the Church abroad by doing voluntary work with overseas churches for periods of up to a year.

USING OUR TIME, TALENTS AND MONEY IN THE
WORK OF THE CHURCH

Each church has its own work to support. Here is some information which may be helpful to members of the Church of Scotland.

The work of the Church of Scotland

A member of the Church of Scotland has three particular responsibilities, to pray for and to support financially the following:

(a) his own church which includes the cost of upkeep, the minister's stipend (or salary) and other expenses;

(b) other churches which cannot pay their minister's full stipend. Help here is given through what we contribute to the Maintenance of the Ministry Fund;

(c) the Mission and Service work of the Church of Scotland.

    Mission—building churches; reaching out to people in hospitals, factories, prisons, colleges and universities; in holiday places and caravan sites; supporting overseas churches in Europe, Africa, Asia and America; Christian Aid, etc.

    Service—homes for children, the elderly, the socially deprived and the mentally handicapped; hostels for young people; moral education; teaching the Christian faith to all age groups; training students for the ministry and full-time Church work at home and overseas.

Information on all this can be found in the Church of Scotland magazine LIFE AND WORK and in PRAY TODAY, an annual guide to the worldwide work of the Church of Scotland.

... and how to give money for this work

Systematic and regular giving of money is the only practical way to support most of this work. The recommended method of giving is by the dated weekly freewill offering envelope. This ensures that you do not forget to contribute on any Sunday when you may not have been able to be 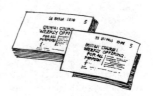 in church. Those who pay tax can greatly benefit their church by making their offering weekly, monthly or annually through a bond of annuity or deed of covenant. Information on this and other financial matters can be had from your church treasurer.

HOW MUCH SHOULD I GIVE?

We can only know what it means to give 'a fitting proportion of our time, talents and money' for the work of the Church if we get our priorities right. Isaiah tells the story of a man who cuts down a tree, uses the greater part of the wood to make a fire on which he can bake bread and with which he can warm himself, and 'the rest of the wood he makes into an idol, and then he bows down and worships it' (*Isaiah* 44:17). The Christian does not worship idols but he does worship God. Are we like the man in the story who thinks first of his own needs and comforts and then gives what is left over to God? For a Christian the priority is to give to God's work first. 'Be concerned above everything else with the Kingdom of God and with what he requires of you, and he will provide you with all these other things' (*Matthew* 5:33).

HOW MUCH MONEY SHOULD BE GIVEN FOR GOD'S WORK?

One day Jesus was sitting near the place in the Temple where people put in their offerings. 'Many rich men dropped in a lot of money, then a poor widow came along and dropped in two little copper coins.' Jesus commended her before the others because 'she had put in all she had – she gave all she had to live on' (see *Mark* 12:41–44).

There is nothing in the Bible about how much we ought to give of money – or of anything else – to the work of the Church. As a starting-point the Jews were expected to give a tithe or a tenth of their annual produce at the beginning of the harvest. Jesus, however, condemned the Pharisee who thought that when he had given his tithe, he had given all that was necessary (see *Luke* 18:12). It is necessary to give a definite proportion of your income to the Church's work but not to regard this as an amount never to be changed. Circumstance may be such that you may want to increase it or to reduce it. The important thing is to give from the heart. 'Each one should give, then, as he has decided, not with regret or out of a sense of duty, for God loves the one who gives gladly' (*2 Corinthians* 9:7).

The fifth vow

DO YOU PROMISE, DEPENDING ON THE GRACE OF GOD, TO CONFESS CHRIST BEFORE MEN, TO SERVE HIM IN YOUR DAILY WORK, AND TO WALK IN HIS WAYS ALL THE DAYS OF YOUR LIFE?

In this vow we are being asked—not on our own but with God's help—to make public acknowledgement of Jesus Christ, to regard our work as a way of serving him, and to live our lives according to his teaching.

CONFESSING CHRIST

Jesus said, 'Whosoever shall confess me before men, him will I confess also before my Father which is in heaven' (*Matthew* 10:32, *AV*). There is no place in the Church for secret disciples. Those who have professed their faith in Christ must be prepared to 'stand up for Jesus'. This is not easy in a society where there is antagonism to the Church, apathy among the membership and a lowering of Christian standards and values.

REAL CHRISTIANS

In countries where the churches do not enjoy religious freedom, it can be dangerous to admit that you are a Christian. In the early days of the Church a Roman consul called Pliny told the Emperor Trajan that he had ordered all Christians to be executed. His test was to get them to deny their faith in public and to curse Christ. Pliny wrote, 'Those who are real Christians cannot be made to do any of these things.'

The apostles, ie those who were 'sent forth' by Jesus were also witnesses to his resurrection (see *Acts* 2:32). A witness was someone who had known Jesus personally and was prepared to acknowledge this in public. The Greek word for 'witness' was 'martus' which means 'martyr'. Many witnesses for Christ became martyrs because of it.

CONFESSING CHRIST

Perhaps the most difficult thing for a Christian to do is to speak about his or her faith to other people. Many members of the Church find it a source of embarrassment to have to mention the name of Jesus in the course of ordinary conversation. A person who has acknowledged him as Lord and Saviour should not be afraid or ashamed to speak of this to others. Here are some ways in which it may be possible for you to do this.

In social contacts

In our everyday life we meet with people who have little or no connection with the Church and who would make no pretence that they are Christians. Use such an opportunity to show where you yourself stand. Close friends will often talk about the deeper things of life. If such an opening is offered to you, do not be like the person who 'lights a lamp and puts it under a bowl'  (*Matthew* 5:15). Let your light shine. Let Jesus be reflected in the person you are and in the words you speak. It will help you if you talk about your faith. 'Be ready at all times to answer anyone who asks you to explain the hope you have in you, but do it with gentleness and respect' (*1 Peter* 3:15).

In house to house visitation

Jesus not only sent out his twelve disciples, he appointed seventy others 'to go ahead of him to every town and place where he himself was about to go' (*Luke* 10:1). The whole Church today is involved in mission. Often this takes the form of a house to house visitation in your local area. Many people are hesitant about becoming visitors in case they are asked questions which they can't answer. On a visitation of this kind the important thing is to be yourself. Speak of what you know. If a difficult question does arise, 'do not be worried about how you will defend yourself or what you will say. For the Holy Spirit will teach you at that time what you should say' (*Luke* 12:12). When you call on someone, pray silently that God will bless that home, and remember that you are there to offer the friendship of Christ and the fellowship of his Church.

CONFESSING CHRIST

This is the story of how Jesus got through to a woman who needed his help. Read the whole of it in *John* 4:1–42. At the time he was passing through Samaria on his way to Galilee. His disciples had gone to a nearby village to buy bread. Jesus was resting at a well – Jacob's Well. A Samaritan woman from the village came to the well to draw water. She had a bad reputation so far as men were concerned and secretly was ashamed of it. In a few moments Jesus had unfolded her life story and was offering his help. She was so thrilled that she ran back to the village to tell everyone about Jesus. Let us look at the method Jesus used to make contact and see where it could help us to make contact with people and so bring them into touch with Jesus.

1. There was a casual meeting. Jesus just happened to be sitting at the well when the woman arrived. Often our first contacts with people are as casual as that.

2. There was a natural conversation. Jesus didn't suddenly say who he was. He asked the woman for a drink of water. From a discussion about water in the well, he pointed her to himself as 'the living water'. We too can approach the spiritual things of life by referring first to the everyday things.

3. There was a simple breaking down of barriers. Not only would it have been unusual for a woman to converse with a man under these circumstances but this woman was a Samaritan and Jesus was a Jew, and there was an age-long hatred between the two races. Jesus removed this barrier by speaking to the woman. To talk to someone when before there has been no communication can be the beginning of the breaking down of barriers.

4. There was a sympathetic understanding of the woman's position. Perhaps Jesus realised that the reason why the woman came to this well which was two miles away from the village was because the other women, knowing her reputation, would not welcome her at the well in the village. In a similar way or through conversation we may be able to discover what someone's real problems are and so be the means of offering that person the help and forgiveness of Jesus.

79

SERVING CHRIST IN OUR DAILY WORK

In the 1980s there are likely to be dramatic changes in the work situation. This is the computer age. The silicon chip has revolutionised our technology. In more and more areas machines have taken over from man and do the same job more efficiently, more economically and more successfully. In turn, this could mean fewer jobs but so far as our attitude to work is concerned, Paul's advice is still valid. 'Whatever you do, work at it with all your heart, as though you were working for the Lord and not for men' (*Colossians* 3:22).

What then does it mean to serve Christ in our daily work?

(1) It means to think of our work as something God has given us to do and which we then do in co-operation with God. There is a story told of Sir Christopher Wren, the architect of St Paul's in London. When the great cathedral was being built, most of the workmen had never seen him. One day he went to visit them on the site. He asked various men, 'What are you doing?' Not knowing who he was, the first said, 'I'm carrying stones.' The next said, 'I'm earning 3/6d a day.' A third replied, 'I am helping Christopher Wren to build St Paul's Cathedral.' For a Christian work is not just a job that has to be done or a means of making money. It is work done for God. 'We are partners working together for God' (*1 Corinthians* 3:9).

(2) It means to think of our work as a form of service to others. So often people work only for their own selfish reasons or they exploit others for personal gain. Jesus said that we must love our neighbour as we love ourselves. For a Christian the important thing is the attitude we adopt towards others. A customer or client is also a brother or sister in Christ.

(3) It means to think of our work as a means of using our talents in God's service. In *Exodus* 35:30 to 36:1 we read of how the builders of the sanctuary gave their skill and craftsmanship for God to use. Whatever abilities God has given us, we must use them in his service and to his glory.

FULL-TIME SERVICE WITH THE CHURCH

When a man becomes a Christian he doesn't have to leave his present occupation. 'Let everyone lead the life which the Lord has assigned to him, and in which God has called him' (*1 Corinthians* 7:17, *RSV*). Nevertheless, God does call certain people to do special work for him. Andrew and Simon Peter, for example, were told by Jesus to leave their nets, to follow him and he would make them 'fishers of men' (*Matthew* 4:19, *RSV*).

IS GOD CALLING YOU TO SOME FULL-TIME SERVICE IN HIS CHURCH?

There are all sorts of opportunities for people who feel that this is what God wants them to do. In most churches the Christian ministry is open to both men and women. Usually this requires a university qualification and the training may last up to six years. There are special courses for older students.

Ministers may be called to a parish at home or to work with the Church overseas. Some do specialised work as chaplains in industry, in hospitals, in universities and colleges, in prisons, in the forces. Some do evangelistic work while others teach religious education.

There are openings for women as deaconesses and for men as lay missionaries. These may be employed in downtown parishes, in new housing areas or in the highlands areas of Scotland.

In the Church overseas there are openings for doctors, nurses, teachers, accountants, builders, agriculturalists, etc. These mainly work in conjunction with local church leaders in the particular country.

Information on careers with the Church may be obtained from the Church of Scotland Offices, 121 George Street, Edinburgh or from the headquarters of other churches.

This is a vast subject covering every area of life. Here we can only look at some of the personal issues that Christians have to face and see what it means to walk in the Christian way.

ALCOHOL

The Bible condemns drunkenness and points out the dangers of excessive drinking.

> 'Don't let wine tempt you, even though it is rich red, though it sparkles in the cup, and it goes down smoothly. The next morning you will feel as if you had been bitten by a snake.'
>
> *Proverbs* 23:31–32

The Bible also says that God provides 'wine to gladden men's hearts' (Psalm 103:13, *NEB*). Paul says, 'Do not drink water only, but take a little wine to help your digestion' (*1 Timothy* 5:23).

For a Christian the standard must be at least moderation and self-control, the ability to say 'Enough and no more!' Some, knowing how difficult this is, would advocate total abstinence. Alcoholism is a serious disease and the only way to avoid it completely is not to touch alcohol at all. Above everything else, don't let your example be responsible for someone else getting a drink problem. 'Decide never to do anything that would make your brother stumble or fall into sin' (*Romans* 14:13).

DRUGS

Drugs can be used for good or for evil purposes. Under proper medical supervision they will give help, comfort and relief to those in pain. Used irresponsibly they can affect the central nervous system and cause irreparable harm.

The soft drugs are either stimulants, sedatives or hallucinogens, ie 'with it' drugs like cannabis and LSD. They may send the user on a 'trip' which can be pleasant at the time but have disturbing after-effects. A drug-taker, once addicted, will almost inevitably turn to hard drugs like morphine and heroin. The cure is a long, painful process and is often unsuccessful.

People who take drugs like this are usually trying to escape from some trouble in their life. Christ does not want us to run away from life but to enjoy it 'in all its fulness' (*John* 10:10).

GAMBLING

Gambling by definition means 'playing games of chance for money'. The moral issue arises when the money is a stronger motive than the game. This is certainly the case with the compulsive gambler but what about the person who buys a raffle ticket to help with some charity? Some would see nothing wrong in this. Others would find no justification for it.

These issues are not resolved by reference to the scriptures. The Bible lays down certain principles regarding our attitude to money. 'Greed', says Paul, 'is a form of idolatry' (*Colossians* 3:5), and again 'the love of money is a source of all kinds of evil' (*1 Timothy* 6:10). The desire for money is certainly encouraged and stimulated by gambling, and the larger the prize the greater is the incentive to win it.

It would be difficult from a Christian point of view to justify gambling when the sole purpose is to get money for nothing. Money is basically something which we receive as a gift, or as payment for goods or services rendered, or as a reward for work done. 'A worker should be given his pay' (*1 Timothy* 5:18). Any other method of getting money is contrary to the teaching of Christian stewardship.

SPEECH

A Christian must be careful both in what he says and in how he says it. The tongue can be 'evil and uncontrollable, full of deadly poison' (*James* 2:8). It has been likened to a fire which sets light to a forest. In no time words can cause infinite harm and hurt.

Swearing – using bad language or dirty words – could be as much a denial of the third commandment (see *Exodus* 20:7) as taking the Lord's name in vain. Swear words are meaningless and lower the tone of a conversation. Nor should it be necessary to bring in God's name to emphasise a point. 'Just say "Yes" or "No"', said Jesus (*Matthew* 5:37). As Christians your speech should be 'pleasant and interesting, and you should know how to give the right answer to everyone' (*Colossians* 4:6).

SEX, LOVE AND MARRIAGE

Love between the sexes is a gift from God. It begins when two people of the opposite sex find pleasure in each others' company. Friendly relationships of this kind are to be encouraged but when a couple fall in love and want to get married, they must recognise that they are then entering into a covenant and that this makes obligations on both of them.

In marriage a husband and wife promise each other lifelong companionship, help and comfort. Marriage, in other words, is a life commitment. Divorce is not a way out for a marriage that may be unsuccessful. No marriage should be entered upon without giving it a great deal of thought beforehand.

Marriage also provides the proper setting for family life. Children should only be born to parents who are able to look after them and bring them up in an atmosphere of love and security. This means that there can be no justification for sexual intercourse outside marriage. Contraceptives are not for the use of anyone who wants to enjoy a sexual experience without any of its consequences. They are for the use of a husband and wife who want to have control over the size of their family.

There is also the problem of marriage between Christians of different religious traditions or denominations. This is one that has to be resolved by agreement between the two people concerned. It is important, for example, that a married couple should be able to worship together in the same church. It is also important that their children should be brought up in a faith that is common to them both. Where a Roman Catholic marries a Protestant, this may not be possible. Young people contemplating marriage with someone from a different religious tradition from their own should consider seriously whether they are doing the right thing if it is going to cause problems for them later on.

SUNDAY-THE LORD'S DAY

For Christians every day belongs to God but Sunday is especially 'the Lord's Day' (*Revelation* 1:10). So far as possible we should regard Sunday as a holy day (holiday) when we can give special thought to God.

How the Lord's Day came to be

Before Jesus' resurrection Saturday was the 'holy day'. According to *Genesis* 1:1–2:4 God created the world in six days and on the seventh (the Hebrew word is *sabbath*) he rested. He stopped working. *Exodus* 20:8–11 states that the seventh day is to be a day of rest when no one is to work.

Some people were so anxious to keep this commandment that they would not even allow 'works of mercy' like making sick people well again. Jesus said that this was to misunderstand the sabbath law. 'The Sabbath was made for the good of man, man was not made for the Sabbath' (*Mark* 2:27). He asked his critics whether the sabbath law was 'to save a man's life or to destroy it' (*Mark* 3:4), and then to show that the sabbath was a day for doing good, he healed people who were sick.

After the first Easter his followers no longer observed the sabbath on the seventh day but on the first day of the week, the day that Jesus rose from the dead. Today most Christians observe Sunday as their sabbath, and as a day for rejoicing.

How the Lord's Day should be kept

(a) A day of worship. Jesus went to synagogue on the sabbath. Christians go to church on Sunday, to celebrate the resurrection of Jesus.

(b) A day of rest. In our modern society not everyone can rest from work on Sundays. We should, however, try on that day to have a change of occupation, to rest from our normal activities. Sunday is a day of recreation, of re-creation.

(c) A day for doing good. Jesus healed people on the Sabbath. On Sunday we should also help people in a special way and so be like Jesus who 'went everywhere doing good' (*Acts* 10:38).

As we come to the last pages of this guide, so we look at those phrases in the Apostles' Creed which we have not yet examined and which have to do with 'last things'.

The Apostles' Creed says:

I BELIEVE IN THE COMMUNION OF SAINTS

The word 'saints' in the New Testament does not refer to people who are specially holy, who have a halo at the back of their heads. It is simply the name given to those who have dedicated their lives to Jesus and who, though they have many faults and failings, are 'called to be God's holy people' (*1 Corinthians* 1:2). In some of the older versions of the Bible they are referred to as 'saints'.

Among the 'saints', however, are also those who have departed this life in the faith of Jesus and who are now like a 'large crowd of witnesses round us' (*Hebrews* 12:1). We do not know who these people are. In *Hebrews* 11 we read that many who died before Jesus came would be included among them. 'Only in company with us would they be made perfect' (*Hebrews* 11:40). It is God who judges whether a person is righteous or not. We must believe simply that we have a close and intimate fellowship, ie communion, with all saints, both those who have accepted Christ here and those who have died in the faith and are now eternally with God.

The Apostles' Creed says:

I BELIEVE IN THE RESURRECTION OF THE BODY

This is a difficult phrase to understand. At death the physical body decomposes in the earth or is dissolved by cremation. Does it all come together again when the body is resurrected? Paul asks a similar question: 'How can the dead be raised to life? What kind of body will they have?' (*1 Corinthians* 15:35). A seed, he goes on to say, is buried in the ground and grows up into a flower. As a flower it has a different 'body' from when it was a seed. When we die, our physical body is raised into 'a spiritual body' because 'flesh and blood cannot share in God's Kingdom' (*1 Corinthians* 15:44, 50). This is what we mean by believing in the resurrection of the body.

The Apostles' Creed says:

I BELIEVE IN THE LIFE EVERLASTING

Life everlasting is not the same as endless existence, which would be no-one's idea of bliss! It is rather a quality of life which never dies and which we can enjoy even in this life. It was about this 'eternal life' that Jesus was speaking when he said, 'I am the resurrection and the life. Whoever believes in me will live, even though he dies; and whoever lives and believes in me will never die' (*John* 11:25).

The Christian, therefore, gives an emphatic 'Yes' to Job's question, 'If a man dies, shall he live again' (*Job* 14:14, *RSV*). And this resurrection life shall have a joyful quality about it. What gave Jesus courage to face death on a cross was 'the joy that was waiting for him' (*Hebrews* 12:2) in his Father's kingdom. He wanted his followers to share in this joy. 'I want them to be with me where I am, so that they may see my glory, the glory you gave me' (*John* 17:24). And Paul confessed that as a Christian he would rather leave his 'home in the body and be at home with the Lord' (*2 Corinthians* 5:8) but he would be happy wherever he was as long as he was serving Christ.

WHAT IS HEAVEN LIKE?

We cannot describe heaven in earthly terms. Jesus says, 'There are many rooms in my Father's house' (*John* 14:2). This is perhaps a description of the size of heaven rather than of its layout. All the biblical accounts suggest that while in heaven we will be 'at home with the Lord', we shall not lose our personal identity or be bored with idleness. The 'rest' which Christians enjoy in heaven is 'to stand before God's throne and serve him day and night' (*Revelation* 7:15).

Death is the reality that all men fear. Job called death 'the king of terrors' (*Job* 18:14, *AV*). We try to soften it with sympathy, flowers and music. The Christian, however, is not afraid of death. He knows that 'neither death nor life... will ever be able to separate us from the love of God which is ours through Christ Jesus our Lord (*Romans* 8:38, 39).

TO HELP YOU READ THE BIBLE . . .

There are many useful modern translations of the Bible, some of which have already been mentioned. These include the GOOD NEWS BIBLE, the NEW ENGLISH BIBLE, the NEW INTERNATIONAL VERSION, the JERUSALEM BIBLE, the LIVING BIBLE (a paraphrase rather than a straight translation), and the more traditional REVISED STANDARD VERSION.

There are also many helpful notes to accompany daily readings and these are graded for different age-groups. SCRIPTURE UNION publishes *Daily Notes, Daily Bread, Keynotes* and *Quest*; THE INTERNATIONAL BIBLE READING ASSOCIATION publishes *Notes on Bible Readings. Light for our Path, Bible Highway* and *Bible Trail*; THE BIBLE READING FELLOWSHIP publishes *Daily Bible Readings, Discovery* and *Compass*; THE SALVATION ARMY has *The Soldier's Armoury* and CRUSADE FOR WORLD REVIVAL has *Every Day with Jesus*. For a commentary on each of the New Testament books there is the late Dr William Barclay's *Daily Study Bible*, published by THE SAINT ANDREW PRESS.

Bibles can be obtained from THE BRITISH AND FOREIGN BIBLE SOCIETY, 146 Queen Victoria Street, London, or THE NATIONAL BIBLE SOCIETY OF SCOTLAND, 7 Hampton Terrace, Edinburgh, or from large booksellers or Christian bookshops. The above notes are also mainly available from these bookshops.